WHAT DO PHILOSOPHERS DO?

THE ROMANELL LECTURES

The Romanell-Phi Beta Kappa Professorship, first awarded in 1983, was established by an endowment from Patrick and Edna Romanell. Patrick Romanell, a Phi Beta Kappa member from Brooklyn College, was H. Y. Benedict Professor of Philosophy at the University of Texas, El Paso. The Phi Beta Kappa Society administers the Professorship, which takes the form of three lectures given each year by a distinguished philosopher, at his or her home institution, on a topic important to an audience beyond professional philosophers. This intent of this series is to publish the results of those lectures in affordable and accessible editions.

Published in the Series

What Do Philosophers Do?
Skepticism and the Practice of Philosophy
Penelope Maddy

WHAT DO
PHILOSOPHERS DO?

Skepticism and the Practice of Philosophy

Penelope Maddy

OXFORD
UNIVERSITY PRESS

OXFORD

UNIVERSITY PRESS

Oxford University Press is a department of the University of Oxford. It furthers
the University's objective of excellence in research, scholarship, and education
by publishing worldwide. Oxford is a registered trade mark of Oxford University
Press in the UK and certain other countries.

Published in the United States of America by Oxford University Press
198 Madison Avenue, New York, NY 10016, United States of America.

CIP data is on file at the Library of Congress
ISBN 978–0–19–061869–8

1 3 5 7 9 8 6 4 2

Printed by Sheridan Books, Inc., United States of America

For J. S. P.
spinner of make-believe

CONTENTS

PREFACE

This book is an attempt to knit together two themes: an investigation of the arguments for radical skepticism about our knowledge of the external world, and an examination of the merits and interrelations of various ways of doing philosophy. The two skeptical arguments that receive the most attention are the Dream Argument and the Argument from Illusion; for completeness, the Infinite Regress of Justification and the Closure Argument are touched on in two short appendices. The methods considered are Commonsense Philosophy, in the person of the Plain Man; Naturalism, in the person of the Plain Inquirer (known in [2007], [2011], and [2014] as the Second Philosopher); Conceptual Analysis; Ordinary Language Philosophy (as practiced by J. L. Austin); and Therapeutic Philosophy (as practiced in different ways by Austin and Ludwig Wittgenstein). Though my own sympathies lie primarily with the Plain persons, I suggest that there's room within their overall approach for productive use of at least some forms of the other methods as well.

The book was drafted in preparation for the Phi Beta Kappa-Romanell lectures, a series commissioned to contribute to 'the public understanding of philosophy'. When the invitation came, I'd been working for some years toward a book on 'Skepticism and the Practice of Philosophy'. It occurred to me that radical skepticism is one philosophical topic that most nonphilosophers have thought about at one time or another and that some discussion of the various methods philosophers use might also appeal to nonphilosophers interested to know more about what philosophy is. When I learned that Peter Ohlin of Oxford University Press had contracted to publish books for a broader audience based on the lectures of the Phi Beta Kappa-Romanell Professors, this raised a puzzle. Should I stick with the original plan for a scholarly book and use the public lectures as a first pass at the material? Should I opt for the more accessible book in place of the scholarly book? Or should I—heaven forbid!—try to sort out two separate books? Unable to resolve this conundrum, I decided just to start writing and see what happened.

In the end, it turned out to be possible—or so it seemed to me, anyway—to say everything I wanted to say in what I hoped was accessible form, that is, without presupposing any background in philosophy. (This isn't to say that readers won't have to don their thinking caps.) The result was the first draft of this book, from which the three lectures were then extracted. I was able to tell part of the story to that audience, but the full story is here. I'm grateful to Phi Beta Kappa for the opportunity to deliver the lectures, to my home institution, the University of California at Irvine, for hosting them, and to OUP for encouraging the longer manuscript.

Much of this material was developed in the course of several extended graduate seminars over the years—on skepticism, naturalism, therapeutic philosophy, philosophies of common sense, theory of perception, conceptual analysis, and ordinary language philosophy. I'm most grateful to the bright and intrepid students who stuck with various of these courses and engaged in lively discussions of the thoughts now set down in this book. And finally, my thanks to David Malament, as always, for his encouragement and so much more.

P. M.

Irvine, California

December 2015

Introduction

Our question is: what do philosophers do? Well, philosophers do lots of things that other people do: I'm up here talking to you much as an English professor or a motivational speaker or a representative of the plumber's union might do. What we want to explore here, more specifically, is what philosophers do *in their capacity as philosophers*, and there again an indisputable answer seems quite ready to hand: they do philosophy. So it might seem more straightforward just to ask what philosophy is, and here often the best answer is to characterize philosophy by giving examples of the kind of questions philosophers tend to ask, questions that don't naturally occur to the rest of us. For example, philosophers ask: what makes 2 + 2 equal to 4?, why is it that a coin that comes up either heads or tails, but doesn't come up heads, *must* come up tails?, how do we come to know anything at all about the world around us? Much of what puzzles outsiders about the philosophical enterprise is the mystery of why a grown person would be drawn to questions like these.

But in fact outsiders aren't the only ones puzzled by what I've just called 'the philosophical enterprise'. Because philosophers are themselves the kind of people moved by at least some of these typically philosophical questions, that part of the subject presents no mystery to them, but they *are* often puzzled, especially in recent years, by the question of method: how should we approach the task of addressing these typically philosophical questions?, is there a special faculty of philosophical insight that philosophers alone employ?, can we learn about the world by some exercise of pure reason?, how does philosophical inquiry relate to scientific inquiry? It's the draw of this range of issues that prompted me to pose our leading question in the form I've given it: what do philosophers do? This is meant to include the implied question of propriety: what *should* philosophers do?, what's the right way to address philosophical questions?, what methods are appropriate and why?

To approach these matters concretely, I propose to focus on the third of the typically philosophical questions floated a moment ago: how do we come to know anything at all about the world around us? And let's begin from a perfectly ordinary point of view, akin to that of Plain Man, a figure who plays a central role in the thought of the mid-20th-century Oxford philosopher, J. L. Austin. When this fellow, the Plain Man, 'look[s] at a chair a few yards in front of [him] in broad daylight',[1] he believes there's a chair there, and though he might

---

1. The quotation is from Austin ([1962] p. 10), where the Plain Man figures prominently in contrast with 'the philosopher' (in this case, A. J. Ayer). He also turns up in Austin [1939] and [1940] (see the final section of Lecture I).

not put it this way, he thereby takes himself to have gained straightforward information about the world, to have come to know something about it. From such simple observations as this of the chair, it's but a small step to modest generalizations, and from there to the threshold of natural science. The late-18th-century Scottish philosopher, Thomas Reid, puts the point this way, early in his *An Inquiry into the Human Mind on the Principles of Common Sense*:

> Wise men now agree, or ought to agree in this, that there is but one way to the knowledge of nature's works; the way of observation and experiment. . . . The man who first discovered that cold freezes water, and that heat turns it into a vapor, proceeded by the same general principles, and in the same method, by which Newton discovered the law of gravitation and the properties of light. (Reid [1765], I.1, pp. 11–12)

So let's imagine Austin's Plain Man imbued with a strong strain of scientific curiosity, intent on investigating every aspect of the world and his place in it, from what you and I would call chemistry and physics, to botany and geography, to anthropology and linguistics, and all points between and beyond—and furthermore, let's imagine him carrying out these investigations by means gradually built up from ordinary observation, through controlled experiment, theory formation and testing, and so on, always circling back to examine and improve those very methods as new information comes to light. Recognizing both her resemblance to the Plain Man and her added inquisitive bent, let's call this person the Plain Inquirer.[2]

So, what does our Plain Inquirer say when asked how she comes to know anything at all about the world? Like the Plain Man, she begins by pointing out that she sees the medium-sized objects around her, along with many of their obvious features, but—tireless investigator that she is—she goes on to explain how the human visual system produces generally reliable beliefs, including accounts of the conditions that tend to facilitate error—fatigue and inattention, low lighting, remote distances or small sizes, and so on—and she points out that these conditions don't hold in the present case. She might even explain why it is that the human visual system works as it does, describing her current best understanding of the evolutionary pressures on our ancestors, how the visual equation was solved differently by different species in different contexts with different survival needs, and so on. Her complete account here will go beyond what's considered the province of any individual science—calling on everything from her understanding of the microstructure of the objects around her, the properties of

2. In other writings (e.g., [2007]), I call this figure the 'Second Philosopher'. I should note that some regard common sense and science, roughly the perspectives of the Plain Man and the Plain Inquirer, as conflicting: e.g., common sense says the table is solid; science says it consists of tiny molecules whizzing around in mostly empty space. It seems to me the Plain Man thinks that the table will support his papers, that his hand won't pass through it, etc.—and of course that's also true of the Plain Inquirer's table. The Plain Man may also have some vague thoughts about how and why the table has these features; he may think the table resists the paper and his hand because there's no space between its parts. If so, then the Plain Inquirer has shown him something surprising about his table, but she hasn't shown (or claimed to have shown) that her table exists and his doesn't. For a bit more, see [2014a].

light and optics, the structure of the eye, the functions of the visual cortex, experimental results on the phenomenal reports of human subjects, even her own visual experiences, past and present—all in the service of arguing that many of her current visual beliefs, like the one about the Plain Man's chair, are very likely to be true. From there, she has even longer stories to tell about the reliability of the principles she uses to generate generalizations, to design experiments, to form and test theories, and so on. I've only described this in the most shorthand, schematic way, but I think you can imagine for yourself that our Inquirer takes herself to know quite a few things about the world and her place in it, and that she has carefully examined and persuasive reasons for believing what she does. She's a thoroughly responsible and successful investigator.

At this point, we might think the philosopher's question has been answered: how do we come to know anything at all about the world around us? Well, the Plain Inquirer replies, we start with ordinary sensory information, which is crafted by evolutionary pressures and works like this, and build up gradually to ever more sophisticated scientific knowledge by carefully confirmed steps so-and-so and such-and-such. Why isn't this the end of the story? What more could the Philosopher want?

In fact, the Philosopher's dissatisfaction at this point isn't just a matter of pure pig-headedness, though it can sometimes appear that way. The source of his dissatisfaction is a range of compelling skeptical arguments that have been offered in various forms at various points in the long history of the subject, arguments that purport to show that we can know nothing about the world, indeed that we have no more reason to believe any one thing rather than any other.[3] These arguments have been discussed, dissected, reformulated, and reexamined, again and again, and though no one has ever been able to truly believe their dramatic conclusion, the arguments themselves have never been conclusively rebutted or removed. This leaves the conscientious Philosopher in the awkward position of simultaneously admitting that he can't help believing that he has hands or that he's standing up or that he's looking at the Plain Man's chair, but at the same time granting that he has no better reason to believe these things than he has to believe their denials. In the course of these lectures, we'll be considering what I take to be the two most compelling of these arguments, to see how they purportedly reach their stunning, skeptical conclusion, to explore how they look from the perspectives of the Plain Man and the Plain Inquirer, and to ask whether the Philosopher sees them differently—and if so, how and with what justification. The hope is that this will leave us with a better understanding of what philosophers do, and perhaps of what they *should* do.

---

3. A terminological note: some versions of 'skepticism' don't go as far as this. A distinction can be drawn between the 'rustic' skeptic, who calls all our beliefs into question, and the 'urbane' skeptic, whose doubts are confined to more theoretical beliefs of one sort or another. I focus here on rustic skepticism because this is the position that presents a direct challenge to the Plain Man. (For these terms, introduced in connection with ancient skepticism (touched on in Appendix A), see Barnes [1982].)

The Dream Argument

1. DESCARTES ON DREAMING

The first of these daunting skeptical arguments is the famous Dream Argument, posed in its original form back in the 17th century by René Descartes at the opening of his *Meditations on First Philosophy*.[1] Descartes meditator[2] begins with the disturbing thought that his apparently well-confirmed system of beliefs may in fact be founded on stubborn errors committed before he had reached the level of full rationality that he now enjoys:

> Some years ago I was struck by the large number of falsehoods that I had accepted as true in my childhood, and by the highly doubtful nature of the whole edifice that I had

---

1. The ancient skeptics also appealed to dreaming, but in a quite different way. For some discussion, with references, see Broughton [2002], p. 68.
2. It isn't clear that the narrator of the *Meditations* should be identified with the author. See Broughton [2002], chapter 1.

subsequently based on them. I realized that it was necessary, once in the course of my life, to demolish everything completely and start again right from the foundations if I wanted to establish anything at all in the sciences that was stable and likely to last. (Descartes [1641], p. 12; AT VII, p. 17)

The challenge, then, is to 'demolish' all his beliefs,

to hold back my assent from opinions which are not completely certain and indubitable just as carefully as I do from those which are patently false. (Ibid., p. 12; AT VII, p. 18)

Recognizing that taking on his beliefs one by one would be an 'endless task', he instead proposes to root them out wholesale, by undermining 'the basic principles on which all my former beliefs rested' (ibid.). Given that 'whatever I have up till now accepted as most true I have acquired either from the senses or through the senses' (ibid.), his goal is to convince himself to reject everything his senses seem to tell him— to reject, that is, the Plain Man's and the Plain Inquirer's starting point.

To accomplish this, it isn't enough just to observe that our senses sometimes get things wrong, that we might easily mistake a distant tree for a house or a straight line for curved in an optical illusion. The Plain Man is well aware of these pitfalls; the Plain Inquirer studies them with care, both in order to guard against them and for the insights they often provide into the actual workings of the visual system. Descartes's meditator, also aware of (at least some of) this, takes up not dubious perceptions like these, acquired in less than optimal circumstances, but perceptions as apparently sound as that of the Plain Man's chair. He then raises and at first rejects a dramatically new turn of thought:

> How often, asleep at night, am I convinced of just such familiar events—that I am here in my dressing-gown, sitting by the fire—when in fact I am lying undressed in bed! Yet at the moment my eyes are certainly wide awake when I look at this piece of paper; I shake my head and it is not asleep; as I stretch out and feel my hand I do so deliberately, and I know what I am doing. All this would not happen with such distinctness to one asleep! (Descartes [1641], p. 13; AT VII, p. 19)

To this point, our Plain persons nod in agreement, but the meditator isn't finished. After claiming 'all this would not happen . . . to one asleep', he makes his fateful rejoinder:

> Indeed! As if I did not remember other occasions when I have been tricked by exactly similar thoughts while asleep! As I think about this more carefully, I see plainly that there are never any sure signs by means of which being awake can be distinguished from being asleep. (Ibid.)

The meditator now glimpses a road to undercutting all his sensory beliefs at once, wholesale:

> Suppose then that I am dreaming, and that these particulars—that my eyes are open, that I am moving my head and stretching out my hands—are not true. (Ibid.)

If this is right, if in fact the Plain persons have no good reason to think they're not just dreaming that they see a chair, then all the Plain Man's protests and Plain Inquirer's careful investigations are powerless to overcome the concern the meditator has just raised.

This may seem damaging enough, but the meditator still isn't finished. He takes himself to have shown that the Plain Man's belief in the chair is 'in a sense doubtful', but holds that it remains a 'highly probable opinion ... much more reasonable to believe than to deny' (Descartes [1641], p. 15; AT VII, p. 22). As we saw at the outset, he wants to withhold his assent from even slightly doubtful beliefs, just as he would from obvious falsehoods; this he feels he must do 'if I want to discover any certainty in the sciences'. Alas, he finds that

> my habitual opinions keep coming back, and despite my wishes, they capture my belief, which is as it were bound over to them as a result of long occupation and the law of custom. (Descartes [1641], p. 15; AT VII, p. 22)

Given that the Plain Man's beliefs are reasonable, indeed 'highly probable', they're quite difficult to unseat. To do this, the meditator takes his final step:

> I think it will be a good plan to turn my will in completely the opposite direction and deceive myself, by pretending for a time that these former opinions are utterly false and imaginary. I shall do this until the weight of preconceived opinion is counter-balanced and the distorting influence of habit no longer prevents my judgement from perceiving things correctly. (Ibid.)

This self-deception is achieved in the first meditation's concluding flourish:

> I will suppose ... some malicious demon of the utmost power and cunning has employed all his energies in order to deceive me. I shall think that the sky, the air, the earth, colours, shapes, sounds and all external things are merely the delusions of dreams which he has devised to ensnare my judgement. I shall consider myself as not having hands or eyes, or flesh, or blood or senses, but as falsely believing that I have all these things. I shall stubbornly and firmly persist in this meditation; and, even if it is not in my power to know any truth, I shall at least do what is in my power, that is, resolutely guard against assenting to any false-hoods, so that the deceiver, however powerful and cunning

he may be, will be unable to impose on me in the slightest degree. (Ibid.)

This has come to be known as the hypothesis of an Evil Demon. Given his power to manipulate every aspect of my experience, it's hard to see how any evidence I might have or obtain could count against his existence. And if I can't rightly convince myself that there is no such malevolent force, how can I be said to know anything at all?

Now as most of you no doubt remember, Descartes's meditator goes on from this apparent catastrophe to argue that he, the thinker, exists (*Cogito, ergo sum*), that there is a benevolent God who wouldn't mislead him, and hence that his senses do give him reliable information about the world. I'll return in a moment to the question of exactly what that reliable information is— and to the sad fact that those who followed Descartes were more shocked by the challenge of the Dream Argument and the Evil Demon hypothesis than they were soothed by his response to it. But before we get to these matters, let's pause a moment to take a first pass at the Plain Inquirer's reaction to Descartes's line of thought. Suppose the meditator confronts her with the possibility that she may just be dreaming that she sees the Plain Man's chair, or that an Evil Demon may be manipulating her experience to make it appear to her that there's a chair in front of her when there isn't. Does this, should this, shake her belief in the existence of the chair?

Notice, first, that the meditator says only that his ordinary sensory beliefs are 'in a sense doubtful', while granting that they are 'highly probable'; in the third meditation he calls the doubt he raises 'very slight' (Descartes [1641], p. 25; AT VII, p. 36) and in other places he describes it as 'extreme' (Descartes [1642], p. 308; AT VII, p. 460) and 'exaggerated' (Descartes [1642], p. 159, 308; AT VII, p. 226, 460). This has led many readers to suppose that this hyperbolic sort of doubt is relevant only because Descartes has an unusually stringent notion of what it takes to know something, because he thinks that knowledge must be absolutely certain. If this is right, then the Plain Inquirer is perfectly free to respond that she never intended to claim that she was certain in any of her well-confirmed beliefs. After all, she recognizes that we're firmly convinced that one line is longer than the other in the familiar Müller Lyer illusion, until we take the trouble to measure them, and that we're momentarily fooled by the stage magician's 'Headless woman', who's really 'a woman against a dark background with her head in a black bag' (Austin [1962], p. 14). Likewise, it could be that someone has taken the trouble to sculpt and paint a chair-like object out of soft clay that will collapse when sat upon or a wooden object of another shape entirely that only looks like a chair from the Plain Man's vantage point. Such opportunities for error can be reduced by further explorations, of course, but the Plain Inquirer is fully prepared to admit that perhaps every one of her beliefs is susceptible to some bizarre sort of error; she's content to conform her beliefs to the best evidence available, to regard them as 'highly probable opinions ... much more reasonable to believe than to deny', in meditator's phrase. (This is called 'fallibilism'.) If the dreaming challenge is just intended to establish this much, then she's in agreement, with no need or grounds to protest.

In truth, though, Descartes's project in the *Meditations* is considerably more interesting than the quixotic pursuit of a misguided ideal of certainty. Descartes was working at the dawn of the scientific revolution, when our investigations of the physical world first took on the empirical, experimental spirit that extends to the present day.[3] Before that, the leading view, the view taught in the schools, was a form of scholasticism derived from Aristotle, according to which objects are pretty much as they appear to common sense. Descartes, in contrast, embraced a new view of the world as mechanical in character, made up of tiny corpuscles with shape, size, and position that combine to form objects. Other conspicuous features, like colors, are only apparent, only sensations in us, not real properties of the objects themselves. By the end of his intellectual journey, the meditator is led to a position compatible with this mechanistic corpuscularism; as the philosophical historian, Janet Broughton, depicts him,

> the meditator . . . will no longer assent to the general belief that things have the colors we see, the warmth we feel, the savor we taste, and so on. . . . He had thought his senses give him knowledge by somehow acquainting him with the very features the objects have. He now realizes that his sense

3. For more on this, in addition to Broughton [2002], see Garber [1986], Hatfield [1993].

perception decomposes without remainder into motions
in his own body that are caused by other bodies . . . he sees
that his awareness . . . corresponds to patterns of changing
shapes and motions in the objects that caused the motions
in his body. (Broughton [2002], p. 198)

Broughton calls attention to this remarkable passage in one of
Descartes's letters:

If an angel were in a human body, he would not have sensations as we do, but would simply perceive the motions
which are caused by external objects, and in this way would
differ from a real man. (Quoted by Broughton [2002],
p. 201)

As she says, we might even suppose that the angel

could rapidly draw inferences from what it knows about the
motions in its human body to the distributions of motions
in the neighborhood of its body. (Ibid.)

In any case, angels aside, if the Plain Man supposes that he sees
a red chair, he is mistaken. This is the world view Descartes is
out to defend.

Described in this way, Descartes's project in the
Meditations doesn't appear to involve any stringent conception of knowledge, so where does the quest for certainty enter
the picture? Why does he feel the need to raise 'slight' and

'hyperbolic' doubt? Broughton gives an elegant and appealing answer to these questions. The problem Descartes faces is that the meditator, at the outset, may well share the Plain Man's (and the Aristotlian's) belief in that red chair he sees, which for now qualifies as 'a highly probably opinion . . . much more reasonable to believe than to deny'; what can Descartes do to undercut a belief he admits to be so well-founded? Returning to the opening strains of the first meditation, we now see why the meditator begins with the worry that his entire system of beliefs may be infected with errors from childhood: those commonsense errors, our beliefs about colors and all the rest, arise very early on, and only afterward make their way into the reigning Aristotelian scholasticism. To unseat them, he needs to find principles even more convincing than they are, principles that are immune even to the 'slight' and 'hyperbolic' doubt to which the red chair belief is subject. The best way to do this would be to find beliefs that are outright certain, and those are what the Method of Doubt is designed to uncover: by first setting aside all beliefs subject to even the slightest doubt, the meditator is in a position to discover the certainties—about his existence, about God, and so on—that can support the new mechanical, corpuscular truths, and thereby falsify even some of the Plain Man's 'highly probable opinions'. In a nutshell: only certainties can effectively trump the senses.

This more subtle reading of Descartes's motivations and goals is considerably more interesting to the Plain Inquirer; it's obviously not enough for her to cheerfully respond that she's fallible. Still, Descartes's procedure does strike her as drastic. She agrees that a fair number of the beliefs she formed in child-hood were false—Santa Claus doesn't exist, appearances can be deceptive—indeed she agrees that some of the Plain Man's beliefs will need adjustment in light of her more sophisticated methods—whales aren't fish but mammals, ordinary objects are mostly empty space—but she thinks that these errors *can* and many *have* been corrected piece-meal, in the course of her steady, thoroughly straightforward inquiry.[4]

Still, Descartes has claimed that his Method of Doubt, the exercise of turning aside all evidence of the senses, will serve as a means to discovering principles more certain than even the most dependable of the Plain Inquirer's current beliefs. It's hard for her to see how this could be so, but she's open-minded and fully prepared to try new methods.[5] The trouble comes in the execution, after Descartes has firmly resolved not to believe the evidence of his senses and proceeds from there to argue that he exists, that God exists, that the essence of body is extension, and so on; these arguments the Plain Inquirer finds unconvincing. So the dis-agreement between them lies there: she doesn't see that

---

4. To be fair, Descartes also had the Church to worry about: Galileo had recently been condemned by the Inquisition for views that Descartes took to follow from his own physics.

5. For the record, some so-called naturalists would reject the Method of Doubt with-out bothering to try it out, on the grounds that it's 'unscientific'. Current philo-sophical use of the term 'naturalism' seems broad enough to include our Inquirer's implicit stance, but she makes no attempt to establish once and for all a fixed dis-tinction between 'scientific' methods and the rest; she simply evaluates each pro-posal individually as it comes along.

employing the Method has the payoffs Descartes claims for it. At that point, she happily returns to her tried-and-true methods and those 'highly probable' beliefs she had before. Notice that neither she nor Descartes has been tempted by any deeply skeptical conclusions: the Method of Doubt is a method, not an argument, to be used or not, depending on its efficacy.

2. STROUD ON DREAMING

The big surprise is that this is not at all the way contemporary philosophers see the situation. For them, the Dream Argument or the Evil Demon hypothesis raise an extremely serious skeptical problem; they pose a genuine and perhaps even insurmountable challenge to our ability to gain reliable information about the world, even to render any belief more reasonable than its denial. If this is right, poor Descartes misunderstood the force of the considerations he himself raises in the first meditation! And again, if this is right, it poses a very real threat to the Plain Inquirer's whole project of coming to understand the world and our place in it. So, why does the Dream Argument now appear so devastating?

The most compelling and influential contemporary presentation of the Dream Argument is due to Barry Stroud, Broughton's senior colleague at UC Berkeley. The stark contrast can be seen in his assessment of Descartes's situation at the end of the first meditation. As we've been understanding the state of play at that point, Descartes regards the Plain Man's belief about the red chair as quite reasonable, mostly likely true, but he has undertaken, as an exercise, to convince himself that all sensory beliefs are false; by this means, he expects to uncover absolutely certain principles that will eventually establish the correctness of some, but by no means all aspects of the Plain Man's belief (the shape of the chair survives, but its color doesn't). Stroud sees the situation quite differently:

> By the end of his *First Meditation* Descartes finds that he has no good reason to believe anything about the world around him and therefore that he can know nothing of the external world. (Stroud [1984], p. 4)

Here it isn't just certainty that's at issue; it's the very possibility of having any good reason at all to believe anything at all about the world, any good reason to believe that there's a chair in front of me rather than that there's not. And this devastating conclusion is said to arise out of Descartes's consideration of the possibility that he is only dreaming that he's sitting by the fire in his dressing gown.

So how is this supposed to work? I assume that all of us—the Plain Man, Descartes, Stroud, and the Plain Inquirer, too—all of us would agree that if I dream that I'm looking at a red chair a few yards in front of me in broad daylight, then I don't thereby know anything at all about a chair or anything else. As he looks at his chair, our Plain Man may well observe,

perhaps with some impatience, that of course he's not currently asleep. The Plain Inquirer's analysis is more elaborate—
she points out as he does that the chair is nearby and that the
lighting conditions are good, but she will also note that various
other potentially distorting factors aren't present in the context or surroundings (no magic show in progress, no obstacles
blocking side views) or in herself (her eyes are open; she's viewing the chair head-on, not out of the corner of her eye, where
color vision is reduced)—but presumably she, too, includes the
observations that she's well-rested (important for clear vision)
and indeed, not asleep! Stroud acknowledges the attraction of
this response:

> Surely it is not impossible for me to know that I am not
> dreaming? Isn't that something I often know, and isn't it
> something I can sometimes find out if the question arises?
> If it is, then the fact that I must know that I'm not dreaming
> if I am to know anything about the world around me will
> be no threat to my knowledge of the world. (Stroud [1984],
> p. 19)[6]

---

6. Sharp-eyed readers will notice a subtle escalation here, beyond the commonplace
observation that if I'm dreaming I don't know: the Plain Man is taking up the
implicit challenge that if he doesn't know he's not dreaming, then he doesn't know
he sees a chair. One school of thought in contemporary epistemology, externalism,
would insist that the Plain Man can know that he sees a chair without being able
to defend that claim, without knowing that he knows. However that may be—it's
taken to hinge on the concept of knowledge, which comes under some suspicion in
the next section—the debate playing out in the text concerns the Plain Man's and
the Plain Inquirer's reasons for thinking they see that chair, their reasons for claiming to know. For more, see Appendix A.

Alas, he continues, 'I think this straightforward response to Descartes's challenge is a total failure' (ibid.).

This response fails, according to Stroud, for the very reason Descartes gives—'there are never any sure signs by means of which being awake can be distinguished from being asleep' (Descartes [1641], p. 13; AT VII, p. 19)—so we need to ask how it is that we ordinarily think we can easily determine whether or not we're awake. Here again, I assume that most of us would offer the same sorts of mundane observations: waking experience is continuous and coherent; my awareness stretches into a long remembered past and forward to my plans and hopes for the future; I can read books, carry on reasonably long trains of thought, execute plans. In contrast, dreaming experience is fragmented and illogical; I'm unable to read or sustain a train of thought or carry out a plan; people and things come and go without rhyme or reason. Descartes's meditator himself cites the same sorts of facts at the end of his intellectual journey:

> There is a vast difference between [being asleep and being awake], in that dreams are never linked by memory with all the other actions of life as waking experiences are. If, while I am awake, anyone were suddenly to appear to me and then disappear immediately, as happens in sleep, so that I could not see where he had come from or where he had gone to, it would not be unreasonable for me to judge that he was a ghost, or a vision created in my brain, rather than a real man. But when I distinctly see where things come from and where and when they come to me, and when I can

connect my perceptions of them with the whole of the rest
of my life without a break, then I am quite certain that
when I encounter these things I am not asleep but awake.
(Descartes [1641], pp. 61–62; AT VII, pp. 89–90)

This is of a piece with what he said in the first meditation,
except that now, after his detour though the existence of God,
and so on, these plain beliefs are purportedly certain, not just
'highly probable opinions': 'in cases like these I am completely
free from error' (Descartes [1641], p. 62; AT VII, p. 90). But
presumably the Plain Man is content with high probability!

The Plain Inquirer adds to these ordinary observations a
wealth of information from her active study of dreaming: she
carefully notes the characteristics of her own episodes of waking and sleeping; she collects data from others about their
experiences; she conducts empirical studies of sleeping subjects, recording their eye movements and brain patterns, and so
on. Some of Austin's notes on the subject take this same form:

> Philosophers are imposed upon at the outset by suppos-
> ing that since the dreamer really thought he was meeting
> the Pope, it must have been just *like* really doing so. . . .
> But there are differences, e.g., in the temporal and spatial
> boundaries. And it is like being told a story: one cannot
> ask for completeness—e.g., what the weather was—if it
> wasn't given. Also . . . things *happen* to the dreamer, often,
> rather than his doing these things. And not only is the sen-
> suous balance different (e.g., few smells), but so also is the

emotional balance quite different in dreams from that of ordinary life. . . . insofar as some people (psychologists) *are* now paying attention to the phenomena of perception, they are discovering that there are many *more* 'qualitative differences' than one ordinary pays attention to (e.g., the work at Cornell). (Austin [1958], p. 8, VII.7; p. 9, VIII.1)[7]

These remarks come from contemporaneous notes of lectures Austin delivered in Berkeley in 1958.[8] The epistemologist Adam Leite brought these notes to wider attention in his paper on Austin's approach to skepticism published in 2011.[9]

Leite is also good enough to provide a helpful summary of the contemporary scientific literature on dreaming: first, on the experiential aside,

dreams are characterized by reduced visual acuity and reduced content in the non-visual sensory modalities

7. In other passages, Austin argues from our meaningful use of the contrast between 'dreaming' and 'waking' ([1946], p. 87) and of the phrase 'dream-like quality' ([1962], pp. 48–49), to the conclusion that we can tell them apart—arguments that at least border on a discredited form known as a 'paradigm-case argument'. Stroud touches on this line of thought but concludes that 'Austin's real opposition to the skeptical philosophical conclusion is to be found elsewhere' ([1984], p. 48). On that much we agree, but (as will come out in section 3) not on where that 'elsewhere' is!

8. Austin [1962] was reconstructed by Warnock from five sets of Austin's notes for lectures delivered between 1947 and 1959; the last of these was prepared for the 1958 Berkeley lectures and used again in 1959. It's unknown why Austin's version of the passage just quoted wasn't included in the book.

9. Grateful as I am to Leite, and much as I admire his paper, my reading here of Austin on skepticism doesn't fully align with his. (E.g., see the text surrounding footnote 3 of Appendix B.)

(including physical sensations such as itches and tickles). One's ability to direct and focus one's attention is significantly hampered ... dreams exhibit distinctive features in their formal structure, including incongruities (strange, unusual, or impossible combinations of elements), indeterminacies of identity and persistence conditions, and fundamental discontinuities in apparent space and time, as well as in the identities of objects and persons. (Leite [2011], p. 83, note 10)

In a dream, the frog really can become a prince! In addition, there are strong neurological correlations between the nature of the experience and the simultaneous brain activity:

REM-sleep ... is a highly unified state of the brain, induced by distinctive changes in the brainstem and characterized by ... [e.g.,] a drastic shift in the relative proportions of [several] neurotransmitters ... a shift which, if produced pharmacologically in a waking person would result in artificially-induced psychosis. ... blood flow to the dorsolateral prefrontal cortex—an area [involved in] planning voluntary activity and in less well-defined functions termed 'executive functions' and 'reality checking'— is reduced roughly by half, in effect shutting down this area to a level adequate only for the preservation of the tissues involved. ... the brain processes signals which appear to be randomly generated by the brainstem and fed to the visual, motor, and emotional systems without 'control' from the systems of the prefrontal cortex. (Ibid.)

All this supports Austin's Plain Man in his conviction that dreaming is quite different from waking and that the differences are clearly discernable.

Let me add that many human subjects (including me) report a phenomenon called 'lucid dreaming'. (The physicist Richard Feynman gives a vivid account of his own experiences in one of his popular books.[10]) In such a dream, the question arises 'am I dreaming?',[11] and the dreamer is able to perform tests to determine the answer: for example, it's often possible to put one's hand through an apparently solid object or to jump much higher than normal, as if in low-gravity conditions; it's impossible to read or to gain stable information from looking at a clock or to turn the lights on and off; sometimes the dreamer can even control the subsequent events in the dream. Research on this phenomenon is only beginning,[12] but studies show that lucid dreaming coincides with blood flow to

10. Feynman [1985], pp. 45–52.
11. As a matter of fact, once the question manages to arise, the dreamer is very close to the realization that the answer is yes.
12. In case it might seem impossible to study such a thing empirically, here is one glimpse of the methods used: 'An experimental advantage is that subjects can signal that they have become lucid by making a sequence of voluntary eye movements. In combination with retrospective reports confirming that lucidity was attained and that the eye movement signals were executed, these voluntary eye movements can be used as behavioral indication of lucidity in the sleeping, dreaming subject' (Voss et al. [2009], p. 1191). Filevich et al. [2015], p. 1082, give further references.

the frontal brain areas intermediate between levels typical of REM sleep and wakefulness.[13] Evidence suggests that if there were anything to be gained by being aware that one is dreaming or by controlling one's dreams, many if not most people could be trained to do it.[14]

With this preponderance of ordinary evidence, from both the Plain Man and the Plain Inquirer, why does Stroud nevertheless maintain that 'the straightforward response is a total failure'? Though he cites Descartes's remark that 'there are never any sure signs', we've seen that Descartes himself takes this to be consistent with there being plenty of good reasons to believe one is awake rather than asleep, even if those reasons fall short of being 'sure' (that is, producing certainty). But Stroud isn't primarily concerned with certainty; he disagrees directly with Descartes, insisting that the Dream Argument leaves us with no better reason to believe than to deny our ordinary beliefs, and our present goal is to figure out what makes him think this. There are hints along the way:

> It is very plausible to say that there is nothing we *could* not dream about, nothing that could be the case that we *could* not dream to be the case. (Stroud [1984], p. 18)

---

13. See, e.g., Voss et al. [2009]. Filevich et al. [2015] suggest a correlation with neural systems typical of metacognition.

14. A pilot study suggests that lucid dreaming may be effective in the treatment of chronic nightmares (Spoormaker and van den Bout [2006]). For evidence that it can be learned, see Zadra et al. [1992].

In fact, we've just seen that this isn't true: for example, I can't get a consistent reading from my wristwatch or successfully consult my smartphone in a dream. For a fresh example, I can't feel thirst in a dream then quench that thirst, because the thirst is real thirst and the water is dream water.

Eventually, Stroud does explicitly raise the question of a test for dreaming:

> Suppose that there is in fact some test which a person can perform successfully only if he is not dreaming . . . (Stroud [1984], p. 21)

First Stroud wonders how we could come to know there is such a test: if I must know I'm not dreaming in order to know anything, then I would have had to know I wasn't dreaming before I knew any of the things on which I base my belief that the test is a good one. There's something a bit funny about this demand: the Plain Inquirer is challenged to defend her Plain Man belief in that chair, but when she tries to do so, she suddenly faces new challenges to each of the beliefs she appeals to in order to answer the first challenge. There is in fact a well-known skeptical argument with this form: what reason do you have to believe p?; answer, q; what reason do you have to believe q?; answer, r; what reason do you have to believe r?, and so on. It appears that I either end with a belief for which I have no reasons or eventually recycle some reason in a viciously circular way (that is, my belief that p ends up being defended on the grounds that p). This is the oldest skeptical argument of them all—the so-called Infinite Regress of Justification—but this isn't the argument we're currently engaged with.[15]

I think Stroud's concern here is actually quite different, not a regress argument at all, and we'll come back to this in a moment, but for now we're fortunate that Stroud himself is happy to set this issue aside: 'suppose we forget about this difficulty and concede that Descartes does indeed know (somehow) that there is a test' (Stroud [1984], pp. 21–22).[16] For the sake of concreteness, let's consider one of the lucid dreamer's tests: can I get a clear and consistent reading of the time by looking at the clock on the wall? Suppose I carry out the test, see that it's 3:05 in the afternoon; I look away, look again, again see 3:05; I conclude that I'm not dreaming. Stroud points out that I would have to know that I carried out the test, and he claims that I can't know this:

> Anything one can experience in one's waking life can also be dreamt about; it is possible to dream that one has performed a certain test . . . And, as we've seen, to dream that something about the world around you is so is not thereby to know that it is so. (Stroud [1984], p. 22)

15. This mode of skeptical argument is discussed in Appendix A.
16. Here again Stroud writes 'a test or circumstance or state of affairs that unfailingly indicates that he is not dreaming', but given that his real interest is in reasonable belief, not certainty, we should just be considering a good test, not necessarily an infallible test.

This must strike us as unfair criticism. To claim outright that I can dream that I see a clear and consistent reading on the clock is just to deny the accumulated facts. That we can't learn the world is so-and-so by dreaming it's so-and-so doesn't undercut the evidence provided by the nature of my dream experience when I look at that clock. Lucid dreaming makes this dramatic, but the same line of thought applies for the Plain Man's more familiar tests: is my experience continuous and coherent?, does it extend into the past and future?, do things come and go in a regular way?

The oddity here traces to that initial remark of Stroud's, quoted a moment ago:

> It is very plausible to say that there is nothing we *could* not dream about, nothing that could be the case that we *could* not dream to be the case. (Stroud [1984], p. 18)

This isn't presented as anything controversial but as an ordinary commonsensical claim. Something similar appears in Broughton's discussion, described there as a plain 'fact of life':

> When I have sense perceptions—that is, when I look at things, or touch, hear, taste or smell them—I am having experience that is indistinguishable by me at the time from some dreams, which are experiences that I have had when I was not having any sense perceptions. (Broughton [2002], p. 77)

Notice the reference here to smell, despite Austin's observation that smells are greatly diminished in dreams: there is in fact no dream experience indistinguishable from my current enjoyment of the strong scent of this rose.

Now Broughton and Stroud are two of the finest philosophical minds I know, so it would be ridiculous to suggest that they're just missing all the obvious and mundane facts I've been surveying here; it's overwhelming likely that they simply regard them as somehow irrelevant. And those of you with a philosophical temperament will probably agree. All along, you may have been inclined to protest: "But the details of how actual dreaming works don't matter! There could be a sort of dreaming that was fully indistinguishable from waking. Your petty complaints about continuity and smells and lucid dreaming are all beside the point, which is about what you could dream *in principle,* and *in principle,* you could be dreaming right now and be completely unable to tell."

Let's pause for a moment to consider how this sort of 'in principle' dreaming might operate. Suppose, for example, that when I go to sleep, on some nights I dream in the ordinary way and on others in this extraordinary way: while dreaming, I have experiences exactly like waking experiences; when I wake up, I find myself in bed and realize that none of what I seemed to experience in the period between going to bed and the present actually happened. If our lives were like this, the Plain Man would no doubt be much more circumspect in his beliefs about that chair apparently in front of him in broad daylight: he would realize that this could be an extraordinary dream; he would realize that he might wake up in a short while and discover that this was just a passing episode of extraordinary dreaming, disconnected with the rest of his life experience. The Plain Inquirer in these circumstances would try to figure out what brings about this sort of dreaming—and perhaps even devise a way for people to detect the state while they're in it. (For example, there might be a characteristic brain pattern; perhaps a detector for this state could be implanted that would produce a mild tickle in the dreamer's left palm as a signal.) Obviously, a population prone to this sort of extraordinary dreaming would be in a much poorer situation than we are when it comes to acquiring reliable information about the world—as philosophers would say, a much poorer *epistemic* situation—but why should this undeniable fact trouble us?

Again, I think the response would be that I've failed to enter into the spirit of the thing. The protest might continue: "It's not a matter of some sort of extraordinary dreaming happening some of the time, occasionally, in the midst of an otherwise continuous and coherent waking life. The idea is that *all* this might be a dream, the whole rigmarole of apparent dreaming and waking, of apparently observing and exploring what happens when people sleep, the entire broader context of your apparently continuous and coherent waking life—for all your know, *all* this might be some larger, overarching dream." *This* sort of extraordinary dreaming, the all-encompassing kind—let's take the term in this sense from now on—this all-encompassing kind of extraordinary dreaming has the same force in practice as Descartes's Evil Demon hypothesis: everything is called into question at once, and the Plain Man is challenged to defend his belief in the chair without appeal to anything else he thinks he knows. The familiar updated version of this type of skeptical hypothesis involves neuroscience fiction:

> Imagine that a human being ... has been subjected to an operation by an evil scientist. The person's brain ... has been removed from the body and placed in a vat of nutrients which keeps the brain alive. The nerve endings have been connected to a super-scientific computer which causes the person whose brain it is to have the illusion that everything is perfectly normal. There seem to be people, objects, the sky, etc.; but really all the person ... is experiencing is the result of electronic impulses traveling from the computer to the nerve endings. The computer is so clever that if the person tries to raise his hand, the feedback from the computer will cause him to 'see' and 'feel' the hand being raised. Moreover, by varying the program, the evil scientist can cause the victim to 'experience' ... any situation or environment the evil scientist wishes. He can also obliterate the memory of the brain operation, so that the victim will seem to himself to have always been in this environment. (Putnam [1981], pp. 5–6)[17]

---

17. Obviously this was written long before the *Matrix* (1999). Notice, also, that the evil machines of the movie aren't as skilled as Putnam's evil neuroscientist: there are discrepancies that allow Keanu Reeves to detect the illusion.

Clearly extraordinary dreaming and its close cousins, the Evil Demon and the Brain in a Vat, all represent a very different worry from the original thought that I might be dreaming in the ordinary, garden-variety sense of the term.[18]

Now suppose we present the Plain Man with this new question: how do you know your belief in that chair isn't part of an extraordinary dream? That is, how do you know you're not just extraordinary dreaming that there's a chair there in front of you in broad daylight? This time the Plain Man can't respond so cavalierly; he can see that the hypothesis of extraordinary dreaming is constructed in such a way that any evidence he might offer could just be part of the same all-encompassing extraordinary dream. Even if he tries to argue that it's very unlikely that he, or anyone else, has ever been subject to an extraordinary dream, he quickly comes to see that any evidence he might appeal to in defense of that likelihood judgment has itself been called into question as potentially part of the same extraordinary dream.[19] The Plain Inquirer will do no better,

---

18. In more recent work, Stroud agrees that the possibility that I might be dreaming is functionally equivalent to the Evil Demon or Brain in a Vat hypotheses, but he denies that the relevant sort of dreaming is what I'm here calling 'extraordinary dreaming' (see also [2007], §1.2, the passage Stroud is responding to): 'It is not that the requirement cannot be fulfilled because some "extraordinary" kind of "dreaming" is in question. It is rather that the requirement cannot be fulfilled when the only resources available are limited to what can be known on the basis of the senses alone' (Stroud [2009], p. 563). This points toward a different style of skeptical reasoning, to be explored in the next lecture. For another way Stroud's argument could work without extraordinary dreaming, see footnote 49.

19. Descartes's position on this point is unclear, at least to me.

though she may note that the differences between the various versions of the hypothesis—extraordinary dreaming, the Evil Demon, the Brain in a Vat—however colorful, are irrelevant to her predicament: all of them boil down to the demand that she defend something or other—the Plain Man's belief about the chair or anything else you might chose—without appeal to any of the tried-and-true, carefully assessed methods that she's developed for finding things out and defending them. She's being asked to produce an entirely new kind of evidence, and she has no idea even how to begin. (Descartes, of course, offered a way out of this predicament, but as we've noted, she doesn't think that it works.)

A while back, Stroud's complaints about the tests for dreaming proposed by the Plain Man and the Plain Inquirer seemed to be degenerating into an infinite regress argument—How do you know p?, Because q., How do you know q?, and so on—with the implication that you can't know anything because the series never ends or runs in a circle.[20] I suggested then that this isn't what's bothering Stroud, that something else is at issue, and we can now see what that something else is: Stroud's skeptic wants a defense of that belief about the chair that doesn't depend on anything else the Plain Man or the Plain Inquirer claims to know, and so in particular, a defense that doesn't depend on facts about how actual dreaming works or the kinds of things that can serve as tests. One way to motivate this demand is an appeal to extraordinary dreaming, and we've

<hr>

20. Again, see Appendix A for more on this style of skeptical argument.

seen that Stroud's characterization of dreaming does lean in that direction.

That Stroud's skeptic is demanding this special kind of defense becomes clearer in his story of the wartime plane-spotters:[21]

> They are given a quick, uncomplicated course on the distinguishing features of different planes and how to recognize them. They learn from their manuals . . . that if a plane has features x, y, and w it is an E, and if it has x, y, and z it is an F. . . . Suppose there are in fact some other airplanes, Gs say, which also have features x, y, z. The trainees were never told about them because . . . it is almost impossible to distinguish an F from a G from the ground. The policy . . . might be justified by the fact that there are not many [Gs] or they are not as directly dangerous as Fs. . . . When we are given this additional information I think we immediately see that even the most careful airplane-spotter does not know that a plane he sees is an F even though he knows that it has x, y, z. For all he knows, it might be a G. (Stroud [1984], pp. 67–68)

Stroud then explains the skeptical challenge by analogy:

> We know that the careful spotter does not know that the plane he sees in the sky is an F. But we can agree that he

---

21. The example is due to Thompson Clarke (see Stroud [1984], p. 67).

does know that according to the manual it is an F. So the question of whether he knows what kind of plane it is is not the same as the question whether he knows what the manual says it is. A reflective airplane-spotter in his spare time might be expected to be aware of that distinction, just as we are. . . . If he does think he knows that some planes in the sky are Fs, he will appeal to the correctness of the manual to explain that knowledge to himself or others.

If it occurred to him that the manual might not be correct, he could see that he was not in the best position he could be in for explaining his putative knowledge. He would see that checking the reliability of the manual would put him in a better position for determining whether what he says when he says 'I know it is an F' is objectively true. It would give him a more objective understanding of his position.

The skeptical philosopher's conception of our own position and of his quest for understanding of it is parallel to this reflective airplane-spotter's conception. It is a quest for an objective or detached understanding and explanation of the position we are objectively in. (Stroud [1984], pp. 80–81)

To spell this out, we can think of the Plain Inquirer as the careful plane-spotter. She believes there's a red chair in front of her because all her well-honed methods of investigating the world tell her this; she also has an account of how these well-honed methods work, what makes them reliable guides, but this account itself relies on elements of her overall beliefs about the world; she doubles back and checks and rechecks these things, as best she can. If this whole evolving package of the Plain Inquirer's beliefs and methods is analogous to the plain-spotter's manual, then in effect, she's using the manual to correct the manual as she goes along. In this way, she *does* investigate the reliability of the manual, but this isn't what Stroud has in mind: the reflective plane-spotter puts the whole of the manual up for examination all at once, not piecemeal. This is what he takes to be required for a 'detached' understanding of our epistemic situation. The claim that we might be extraordinary dreaming—or subject to the machinations of the Evil Demon or the neuroscientist with our Brain in a Vat—these various claims serve to point us toward precisely this philosophical goal: to successfully rule it out would be to justify our beliefs 'from scratch', without appeal to anything else we think we know, it would be to provide just the 'detached' understanding that Stroud's skeptic is after.

At this point, the skeptic's question has been clearly distinguished from the kinds of questions the Plain Man and the Plain Inquirer typically ask, despite the fact that these questions are often expressed in precisely the same words: 'What evidence do you have, what reason do you have to believe, that there's a chair in front of you?' The skeptic's question is much like the one Descartes raises at the end of the first meditation: how can we justify our beliefs without appeal to our usual ways of justifying beliefs?[22] And we've seen that neither the Plain Man nor the Plain Inquirer makes any claim to be able to meet *this* challenge! Still, they can't help wondering why their inability to produce the extraordinary kind of evidence being demanded—evidence that doesn't employ any of their ways of gathering evidence—why their failure to produce this extraordinary kind of evidence serves to invalidate all the ordinary evidence they have and are prepared to provide in great quantity. They can't achieve the kind of certainty that Descartes is after, or the kind of detached overview that Stroud's skeptic is after, but they remain confident that they can achieve 'highly probably opinions', which is enough for them.

So, if our inability to answer the philosophical challenge is to have the dire consequence that our everyday beliefs—and the scientific beliefs that grow out of them—are all no more likely than their denials, then we need to know more about how the philosophical standards relate to the everyday and scientific standards; we need to know why the 'detached' standards somehow overrule the ordinary ones. This is a question that Stroud considers at length. His central claim is that the skeptic's requirement that extraordinary dreaming be ruled out is actually implicit in our ordinary standards, despite the acknowledged fact that it isn't enforced in practice. If this is right, if ruling out extraordinary dreaming is really of a piece with the Plain Man's and the Plain Inquirer's very own ways of

---

22. Though not exactly like, as will come out in the final section of next lecture.

finding out about the world, if this requirement arises out of the very methods they both apply every day, then this is a challenge they cannot simply set aside as irrelevant to their investigations of the world; it's a challenge they must meet if they hold out any hope of confidence in beliefs supported by their very own standards.

Stroud's skeptic's support for this frightening claim begins from the simple fact of our natural reaction to Descartes's reasoning:

> One thing the sceptical philosopher can appeal to to show that he does not introduce a new or extraordinary conception of knowledge [or evidence][23] . . . is the ease with which we all acknowledge, when presented with the case, that Descartes ought to know that he is not dreaming if he is to know that he is sitting by the fire with a piece of paper in his hand. The force we feel in the sceptical argument when we first encounter it is itself evidence that the conception of knowledge [and evidence] employed in the argument is the very conception we have been operating with all along. (Stroud [1984], p. 71)

Of course it may well be that what presents itself to us as obvious is the requirement that we be able to rule out ordinary

---

23. Stroud speaks of 'knowledge' here, but I assume he intends the same considerations to show that, for example, the notions of 'evidence' and 'reasonable belief' involved are also just our ordinary ones. This difference will return later but can be safely ignored for now.

dreaming, which, as we've seen, we can do. The requirement that we be able to rule out extraordinary dreaming is another matter entirely. Perhaps the reasoning goes down so easily because there's an unnoticed shift between the obvious need to rule out ordinary dreaming at the beginning and the impossibility of ruling out extraordinary dreaming at the end. Those of philosophical temperament often shift to 'in principle' almost without noticing!

3. STROUD VERSUS AUSTIN

But Stroud has more than this to say on why the skeptic's philosophical challenge is implicit in our everyday methods; most conspicuously, he engages in an extended tussle with Austin, the Plain Man's friend. Austin is especially important for our methodological purposes here because he employs several distinct and distinctive approaches to the practice of philosophy. We've already seen one of these in his appeals to the Plain Man; this so-called 'philosophy of common sense' is also present in the work of Thomas Reid (from whom we've already heard some and stand to hear more) and of Austin's elder contemporary, the Cambridge philosopher G. E. Moore (who'll be another of our recurring figures).[24] A second arrow to Austin's quiver will emerge in the next lecture, but the one

24. Scholars speculate that Moore was influenced by Reid, and that this influence passed from Moore to Austin, but the evidence is circumstantial.

relevant right now is a third, what's come to be called 'ordinary language philosophy'.[25]

Here Austin begins from the conviction that the language we speak, the language of the Plain Man, is a precision instrument honed over many generations, much more powerful and subtle than philosophers tend to realize:

> Our common stock of word embodies all the distinctions men have found worth drawing, and the connexions they have found worth marking, in the lifetimes of many generations: these surely are likely to be much more numerous, more sound, since they have stood up to the long test of the survival of the fittest, and more subtle, at least in all ordinary and reasonably practical matters, than any that you or I are likely to think up in our arm-chairs of an afternoon. (Austin [1956], p. 182)

So he proposes that 'at least . . . *one* philosophical method' is to

> proceed from 'ordinary language', that is, by examining *what we should say when,* and . . . why and what we should mean by it. (Ibid., p. 181)

Writing in the 1950s, at Oxford, where his strong influence had recommended this approach to many, he sounds notes of both confidence and caution:

---

25. Reid is also a precursor of ordinary language philosophy. For more, see footnote 35 of Lecture III.

> Perhaps this method ... scarcely requires justifica-
> tion at present—too evidently, there is gold in them thar
> hills: more opportune would be a warning about the care
> and thoroughness needed if it is not to fall into disrepute.
> (Ibid.)

Alas this concern was prophetic, as ordinary language philosophy has fallen very far into disfavor since then, at least partly
(it seems to me) as a result of insensitive application by thinkers considerably less rigorous than Austin. (I once asked a keen
observer's opinion on why ordinary language philosophy is
so widely dismissed these days. The reply came: there wasn't
any school of ordinary language philosophy, there was just one
genius.[26]) Like Stroud, our focus here is on Austin's own thinking, so we leave the rest of the loosely connected ordinary language 'school' to fend for itself.

Central among the warnings and cautions Austin raises is
this one:

> Ordinary language ... embodies, indeed, something bet-
> ter than the metaphysics of the Stone Age, namely, as was
> said, the inherited experience and acumen of many genera-
> tions of men. But then, that acumen has been concentrated
> primarily upon the practical business of life. If a distinction
> works well for practical purposes in ordinary life (no mean

---

26. The author of this clever remark prefers to remain anonymous because, of course,
it's an exaggeration. For just one illustrative example of a contemporary philosopher doing valuable work in an Austinian tradition, see Baz [2012].

feat, for even ordinary life is full of hard cases), then there is
sure to be something in it, it will not mark nothing: yet this
is likely enough to be not the best way of arranging things
if our interests are more extensive or intellectual than the
ordinary. (Austin [1956], p. 185)

The method of 'what we would say when' is emphatically not
recommended for all areas of inquiry:

> Using . . . such a method, it is plainly preferable to investi-
> gate a field where ordinary language is rich and subtle, as it
> is in the pressing practical matter of Excuses, but certainly
> is not in the matter, say, of Time. (Ibid., p. 182)

One conspicuous difference here is that Time, unlike Excuses,
is subject to scientific investigation. The quotation above that
recommends against the method when 'our interests are more
extensive or intellectual than the ordinary' continues by noting that our 'inherited experience'

> . . . has been derived only from the sources available to
> ordinary men throughout most of civilized history: it has
> not been feed from the resources of the microscope and its
> successors. (Ibid., p. 185)

In these passages and others like them, Austin clearly indicates
that ordinary language analysis is only appropriate in a certain
kind of case, like excuses. Scientific investigation is not only

the right method for other cases, like time, but also a much-needed supplement even when ordinary language considerations *are* relevant:

> In spite of the wide and acute observation of phenomena
> of action embodied in ordinary speech, modern scientists
> have been able, it seems to me, to reveal its inadequacy
> at numerous points, if only because they have had access
> to more comprehensive data and have studied them with
> more catholic and dispassionate interest than the ordinary
> man . . . has had occasion to do. (Austin [1956], p. 203)

His examples are displacement behavior[27] and compulsive behavior.[28] In general, then, unlike some other practitioners of the art, Austin fully recognizes that

> certainly, then, ordinary language is *not* the last word: in
> principle it can everywhere be supplemented and improved

27. See Austin [1956], pp. 203–204: 'Observation of animal behavior shows that regularly, when an animal is embarked on some recognizable pattern of behavior but meets . . . with an insuperable obstacle, it will betake itself to energetic, but quite unrelated, activity of some wild kind, such as standing on its head . . . If now, in light of this, we look back at ordinary human life, we see that displacement behavior bulks quite large in it: yet we have no word, or at least no clear and simple word, for it. If, when thwarted, we stand on our heads or wiggle our toes, then we are not exactly *just* standing on our heads, don't you know, in the ordinary way, yet is there any convenient adverbial expression we can insert to do the trick? "In desperation"?' A familiar example is scratching our heads or chewing on our pencils when we can't figure something out.

28. Recall also the reference to dream research at Cornell (on p. 23).

upon and superseded.[29] Only remember, it *is* the *first* word. (Ibid., p. 185)

Though Austin's most focused discussion of our knowledge of the world was written before the explicitly methodological remarks we've been reviewing, he applies something very like this approach to the case of the word 'know'. He begins by observing that when I say 'there is a goldfinch in the garden', or the Plain Man says 'there's a chair in front of me', 'we are liable to be asked, "How do you know?"' (Austin [1946], p. 77). This question

> may well be asked only out of respectful curiosity, from a genuine desire to learn. But again, [it] may ... be asked as [a] *pointed* question ... [which] suggests that perhaps you *don't* know it at all. ... If the answer ... is considered unsatisfactory by the challenger ... his next riposte will be ... something such as 'Then you don't know any such thing', or 'But that doesn't prove it: in that case you don't really know it at all'. (Ibid., p. 78)

Of course this is just the outcome of the Plain Man's dialogue with the skeptic, but Austin's intent at this point is to examine how this sort of exchange unfolds in ordinary life—and to what end.

---

29. Indeed, 'superstition and error and fantasy of all kinds do become incorporated in ordinary language and even sometimes stand up to the survival test (only, when they do, why should we not detect it?)' (Austin [1956], p. 185).

Suppose my very British friend is visiting Southern California. To give him a dose of local color, I take him to the ocean; we're standing on a bluff above the beach watching the surfers, a scene I imagine to be unique in his experience. After a few minutes he causally remarks that one of the local surfers is riding a particularly innovative board (suppose he's right about that). I'm naturally amazed at this and immediately ask, 'How you do know?' This might well count as one of Austin's pointed questions, since it seems to me so unlikely that this fellow *would* know such a thing. To my surprise, he responds that he has long maintained a subscription to a leading California-based surfing magazine which he reads cover to cover every month, and he recently read therein about these particular boards. When I grant that this response is satisfactory, when I admit that he does know, I'm acknowledging that he is in a position to make such judgments reliably. I'm using 'he knows' to distinguish him from the vast majority of his countrymen, who haven't taken the opportunity to familiarize themselves with the various types of surfboards.

Now suppose, on the other hand, that he responds to my challenge by saying, 'I got a good look at it as he was carrying it down to the beach'. That wouldn't be satisfactory, because it would leave open my main concern: that he hasn't lived in conditions that would prepare him to judge surfboards. On the other hand, if I were standing on that bluff with a regular surfer at that beach and he were to make the same remark about an innovative board, my pointed question might be prompted by the fact that we were viewing the surfers from such a great distance that it seemed unlikely he could discern the details of the board's design. In that circumstance, 'I saw an article in last month's *Surfing*' or even 'My friend Sally has one of those boards' wouldn't be satisfactory. It would establish that he'd lived in conditions that would prepare him to make the judgment, but that wasn't my concern. A satisfactory answer in this case would be the very one that was unsatisfactory from the Englishman: 'I got a good look at it as he was carrying it down to the beach'.

On a different occasion, the relevant factor might be not training or opportunity, but the actual criteria applied to form the judgment when the board was viewed on its way down to the beach. Under these conditions, a satisfactory response to 'how did you know?' might be 'these new boards have a distinctive shape'—if I trust him as an expert, I'll say he knows. If I myself am also an expert, he might respond instead, 'it's one of Al Merrick's new hybrid shapes', or even, as we now watch the surfer from above, 'that's how he's getting those tight-arc turns and still planing through the flats'.[30]

The point of all this is that an exchange involving 'know' can be used to challenge various aspects of a knowledge claimant's credentials and that we're quite adept at figuring out what kind of thing is in question at the moment and answering accordingly. Still, complex and varied as these functions of 'know' may be, they're nowhere near the end of the story: for example, we haven't inquired into the cogency of the particular evidence the claimant cites. Returning to Austin's own

---

30. Thanks to lifelong surfer Aaron James for his help with this example.

example of the goldfinch in the garden, I might respond to 'How do you know?' with various factual claims:

> 'From its behavior', 'By its markings', or, in more detail, 'By its red head', 'From its eating thistles'. That is, I indicate, or to some extent set out with some degree of precision, those features of the situation which enable me to recognize it as one to be described in the way I did describe it. (Austin [1946], p. 83)

Here again a range of different challenges might be lodged: that goldfinches don't have red heads; that lots of other birds have red heads, too; that the features I've listed better describe a goldcrest. And beyond these concerns about the bearing of the facts I've cited on the question of correctly identifying the bird, there a lies another range of challenges to the purported facts themselves:

> Is the head really red? . . . isn't there perhaps an odd light reflected on it? . . . are you certain it's the right red for a goldfinch? Are you quite sure it isn't too orange? Isn't it perhaps rather too strident a note for a bittern? (Ibid., p. 86)

And so on.

From a wealth of observations like these, Austin draws a few general morals. One of these is that a challenge 'that's not enough', as in 'just having a red head isn't enough', must come with 'some more or less definite lack', for example, because 'woodpeckers have red heads too' (Austin [1946], p. 84). Otherwise, 'it's silly (outrageous) just to go on saying "That's not enough"' (ibid.). Another is that

> enough is enough: it doesn't mean everything. Enough means enough to show that (within reason, and for present intents and purposes) it 'can't' be anything else . . . it does not mean, for example, enough to show that it isn't a *stuffed* goldfinch. (Austin [1946], p. 84)

The thought is that there must be some special reason to think the identified 'lack' might be present in this case. In ordinary conditions, though 'it might be stuffed' is a 'a definite lack', it's absurd to worry about it. But if I live next door to a practical-joking taxidermist, it might well be a good idea to check.

There's much more in Austin's rich discussion, but this should give a sense of his procedure. What he's done is to lay out for us some of the many practices we engage in with the simple word 'know'; we come away with a better appreciation of its surprisingly subtle role in our dealings with the world and our fellows. Often in cases like this, Austin's goal is to marshal enough plain facts of usage to convince us

> that the distinctions embodied in our vast, and for the most part, relatively ancient stock of ordinary words are neither few nor always obvious, and almost never just arbitrary. (Austin [1962], p. 63)

In this case in particular, he hopes to have shown that the word 'know'—dating back to Middle English, with roots back to Latin and Greek—is actually quite an effective expressive tool, eminently useful and finely honed.

So, what does Stroud's skeptic have to say in the face of all this? He begins by noting that the skeptical argument does introduce 'a definite lack'—namely, the possibility that the Plain Man might just be dreaming he sees a chair in front of him—so it doesn't represent an exception to Austin's first general conclusion about our ordinary practices with the word 'know' (see Stroud [1984], p. 46). This leaves open the second condition, that there be a special reason to suppose that I might be dreaming. Here Stroud openly admits that

a moment's reflection seems enough to convince us that Descartes's condition is not in fact a condition of knowledge in everyday or scientific life. After thinking about philosophical skepticism for some time we often tend to forget or distort what we actually do in everyday life, but if we insist on returning to a realistic account of how we actually behave there seems little doubt that we do not in fact impose that general condition on our knowledge-claims. (Stroud [1984], pp. 48–49)

If I testify on the witness stand that I spent the day with the defendant, that I went to the museum and then had dinner with him, and left him about midnight, my testimony under normal circumstances would not be affected in any way by my inability to answer if the prosecutor were then to ask 'How do you know you didn't dream the whole thing?'. The question is outrageous; it has no tendency to undermine my knowledge. It is nothing more than the desperate reaction of a hard-pressed lawyer with no case. Nor do we ever expect to find a careful report of the procedures and results of an elaborate experiment in chemistry followed by an account of how the experimenter determined that he was not simply dreaming that he was conducting the experiment. No such thing was in question; the issue is never raised, let alone settled. (Ibid., pp. 49–50)

In neither case is there a special reason to worry that I might be dreaming, so, the Austinian line of thought is taken to suggest, the question needn't be raised.

Before we examine Stroud's response to this, notice that the dreaming in question here must be extraordinary. If it were ordinary dreaming, then I could easily explain that my recollection of the day I spent with the defendant is quite detailed, entirely continuous and coherent, nothing like the recollection of a dream experience; likewise the chemist, if called upon to do so, could provide abundant evidence that the experiment wasn't dreamt. If ordinary dreaming is in question, then Stroud's description is off: it isn't that I'm not called upon to answer this particular challenge to my testimony, or the chemist to include that appendix, because it would be too difficult for us to do so; those extras aren't requested or provided because they're too obvious to be worth asking about or stating! On the other hand, if the dreaming in question is extraordinary, then what Stroud says is true: neither the Plain Man on the witness stand nor the Plain Inquirer in the chemistry lab would be able to turn that possibility aside, yet we would find it 'outrageous' if they were asked to do so.

Now Stroud has no intention of questioning these home-spun observations about our practices with the word 'know':

> I ... want to grant everything Austin says about what sort of thing does actually happen when ordinary people are asked 'How do you know?', and everything else that could be discovered about how we respond to questions or would-be challenges of others with respect to our knowl-edge. (Stroud [1984], p. 53)

What concerns him is the purported connection between these observations and the skeptical reasoning, which he sees this way: since the lawyer doesn't ask me to show that I wasn't dreaming, since the chemist doesn't include an appendix to his report that rules out dreaming, it must be that 'our everyday procedures and standards' (ibid.) don't actually require us to rule out the possibility that we're dreaming. (Again the dream-ing in question here has to be extraordinary, for the reasons just noted.) Stroud thinks that this purported connection is spurious, that the demand that extraordinary dreaming be ruled out is of a piece with 'our everyday procedures and stan-dards', despite the obvious fact that it isn't actually enforced in our day-to-day dealings.

How can this be? Stroud calls attention to

> our ordinary conception of knowledge ... a conception
> of knowledge that we employ in everyday life prior to and
> independently of all philosophizing. (Stroud [1984], p. 55)

What Austin gives us is 'facts of speech, of linguistic usage'
(ibid., p. 56). Stroud's thought is that those facts of speech and
usage may not perfectly reflect the true contours of the everyday concept:

> It is admittedly bizarre, silly, outrageous, perhaps even
> incomprehensible, to raise the dream-possibility as a criti-
> cism of ordinary claims to know things in everyday and
> scientific life, but exactly what kind of outrageousness or
> inappropriateness is it? ... Is anyone who raises the possibil-
> ity in normal circumstances necessarily violating or reject-
> ing the everyday meaning of the world 'know'? (Ibid., p. 57)

(Note the shift here from 'the everyday concept' to 'the everyday
meaning'. As we'll see, these are often taken to be interchange-
able.) The point is that an utterance can be 'outrageous'—in
the sense of inappropriate or impolite or in some other way a
violation of conversational norms—without being false.

This idea comes from Paul Grice, an Oxford philosopher
who joined Stroud at UC Berkeley in 1967, immediately after
having delivered, at Harvard, the William James lectures that
grew into the book of interest to us here. Though Grice's work

is often cited as the deathblow to ordinary language philoso-phy,[31] he didn't see it this way himself:

> Some of you may regard some of the examples . . . I am about to mention ['perhaps the most interesting and puzzling' of which come from Austin (Grice [1967], p. 8)] as being representa-tive of an outdated style of philosophy. I do not think that one should be too quick to write off such a style. (Grice [1967], p. 4)

Grice very much admires Austin, to whom he sometimes refers as 'the Master',[32] but he worries about phenomena like this:

> Suppose that A and B are talking about a mutual friend, C, who is now working in a bank. A asks B how C is getting on in his job, and B replies, 'Oh quite well, I think; he likes his colleagues, and he hasn't been to prison yet'. (Ibid., p. 24)

Supposing that both A and B know C to be a perfectly honest fellow, this is a very odd, perhaps even 'outrageous' thing for B to say. It isn't that it's false, of course, but it violates a certain norm of conversation, namely the convention not to say more than is needed. Violating this particular norm introduces con-fusion into our cooperative conversational endeavor:

> There may be an indirect effect, in that the hearers may be misled as a result of thinking that there is some particular *point* in the provision of excess information. (Ibid., p. 27)

---

31. See, e.g., Soames [2003], Part Four.
32. Grice [1987], p. 182, though the context is 'if the Master wobbles thus, what should we expect from his friends ... ?'.

Indeed, B starts to wonder if A has some reason to doubt C's honesty (ibid., p. 31)![33]

Grice gives a fascinating taxonomy of such norms and the consequences of their violation, but the upshot for our purposes is precisely Stroud's point: its being outrageous to ask the testifying Plain Man or the experimenting chemist to show that he's not extraordinary dreaming before he claims to know doesn't by itself imply that he does know even without having satisfied that requirement. Grice takes his observations to be reason for the ordinary language philosopher to proceed with care; indeed, he hopes to construct

a theory which will enable one to distinguish between the case in which an utterance is inappropriate because it is false ... and the case in which it is inappropriate for reasons of a different kind. (Grice [1967], p. 4)

General theory or not, this caution seems of a piece with Austin's own warnings, and well within the scope of studying 'what we should say when, ... why and what we should mean by it' (Austin [1956], p. 181).

---

33. Another notable example is 'damning with faint praise' (see (1a) on p. 33 of Grice [1967]): I say that a job candidate has neat handwriting; the conversation norm to 'make your contribution as informative as is required (for the current purposes of the exchange)' (ibid., p. 26) is violated—unless of course my goal is actually to imply that she has no more substantial virtues! The identification and study of this kind of implication, called 'conversational implicature', is one of Grice's most original and influential contributions.

In any case, Stroud's contention is this: it may be true that the Plain Man doesn't know where the suspect was unless he knows he wasn't extraordinary dreaming; it may be true that the chemist's lab report isn't good enough to support his knowledge claim without the relevant appendix; but it might still be inappropriate, even 'outrageous' to criticize either of them on these grounds, given that they've made their claims under just about the best conditions, with just about the best evidence a human being can have for claiming to know something:

> [T]he requirement that there must be some 'special reason' for thinking a certain possibility might obtain in order for that possibility to be relevant to a particular knowledge-claim would be seen as a requirement on the appropriate or reasonable assertion of knowledge, but not necessary as a requirement on knowledge itself. (Stroud [1984], p. 63)

So the question becomes: what reason is there to think that the everyday concept and our linguistic practices *do* in fact diverge in this way?

Stroud's answer[34] involves a distinction between practical and theoretical contexts:

> The standards or procedures we follow in everyday life find their source in the exigencies of action [where] truth is not

---

34. More precisely, Stroud's skeptic's answer. Stroud's goal here is to lay out the skeptical reasoning as persuasively as he can, not to endorse it.

the only important consideration.... It would be silly
to stand for a long time in a quickly filling bus trying to
decide on the absolutely best place to sit. Since sitting
somewhere in the bus is better than standing, although
admittedly not as good as sitting in the best of all possible
seats, the best thing to do is to sit down quickly. (Stroud
[1984], p. 65)

Checking our beliefs or justifying our claims to know
something is itself something we do.... It is a practical
question how much time, effort and ingenuity we should
spend on [this], so we might easily find that it would be
silly or outrageous on a particular occasion to go on trying to eliminate a certain possibility. That is to say, it would
silly or outrageous in the circumstances to act in that way.
(Ibid., p. 66)

So Austin may well be right that our inherited linguistic practices with the word 'know' are well-hewn, subtle and effective, but they still may diverge from 'our ordinary conception
of knowledge' because those practices are also shaped by
practical limitations of time and resources. If we examine our
evidence from a theoretical perspective—that is, at our lei-
sure, with all the resources we need, exercising maximal care
and thoroughness—if we refuse to cut corners in the ways
we do under practical pressures, we realize that we don't in
fact know what we ordinarily and quite appropriately say we
know.

I think there are several reasons for dissatisfaction with this line of thought, beginning with what seems to me a mischaracterization of Austin's overall strategy. The trouble lies in the very notion of 'our ordinary concept of knowledge'. For this concept or (as we noted in passing) 'the meaning of the word "know"' to play the role Stroud suggests, they would have to enjoy some determinate features all on their own, independently of our linguistic practices. Stroud makes this point dramatically by first sketching in

[t]he idea that the world is there quite independently of human knowledge and belief . . . things [are] a certain way whether anyone is affected by them or interested in them or knows or believes anything about them or not. (Stroud [1984], p. 78)

Consider, for example, the claim that 'there is a mountain more than five thousand metres high in Africa'.

[This is] true, or false, depending solely on the heights of the mountains in Africa. Whether anyone knows or believes or has any special reason to suspect anything about those mountains is not part of what I believe when I believe there is a mountain more than five thousand metres high. If I do not know what to believe and I ask or wonder whether there are any mountains in Africa more than five thousand metres high, my question has an answer which is completely independent of anyone's knowing or believing

or being in a position to assert anything. It is quite independent of whether any human or other animate beings
have ever existed. What I ask or come to believe concerns
only the distance above sea-level of certain mountains.
(Ibid., p. 77)

Having lulled us into complacency with these 'platitudes'
(ibid., p. 76), he moves on to knowledge claims.

Many of the things we ask or believe or want to know about
. . . involve human knowledge, human belief and human
reasoning. We ask whether anyone knows . . . that sitting in
a draught contributes to catching cold, and if so how they
know it. . . . They are questions about what we might call
the human world, as opposed to that non-human part of
the world that would have been the way it is whether any
human beings had existed or behaved in certain ways or
not. (Ibid., p. 78)

And now comes the critical step:

Even here, I think, with respect to knowledge . . . we have
the same conception of objectivity. We want to know
whether it is objectively true that somebody knows . . . that
sitting in a draught contributes to catching a cold. . . . facts
of human knowledge . . . are . . . as objective and as independent of anyone's knowing what they are as are the facts
about mountains in Africa. (Ibid., pp. 78–79)

'Knowledge', or the relation of people to facts that counts as 'knowing', is a feature of the world as objective as many others.

This is not a minority view. For many decades now, much of the effort of epistemologists (that is, philosophers concerned with human knowledge) has been directed toward discerning the shape and content of the concept of knowledge. Contemporary readers of Austin, apparently including Stroud, often take him to be engaged in this project as well, to be specifying some or all of the conditions that must be satisfied in order for someone to know[35]—conditions, Austin is understood to claim, potentially less demanding than some others would have it. But I think Austin's oblique message is more radical than this.[36] Let me explain.

When Austin was writing, Moore and others[37] had recently introduced a revolutionary new vision of philosophical method, the idea that a large part, if not all, of the philosopher's job is the careful analysis of the content of concepts like 'cause', 'freedom', and in our case, 'knowledge'. Moore believes that if this were done attentively enough, 'many of the most glaring difficulties and disagreements in philosophy would disappear' (Moore [1903], Preface). This is not to be confused with defining a word, or with Austin's project of asking 'what we should say when':

---

35. E.g., Lawlor [2013].
36. Stroud may lean in this direction himself in later remarks on Austin (e.g., see his [1996], pp. 136–137).
37. Frege is often, and Russell nearly always, cited. Russell reports, 'It was toward the end of 1898 that Moore and I rebelled . . . Moore led the way, but I followed closely in his footsteps' (Russell [1959], p. 42). Frege's concerns were somewhat different.

A definition ... often mean[s] the expressing of one word's meaning in other words. But this is not the sort of definition I am asking for. Such a definition can never be of ultimate importance to any study except lexicography. If I wanted that kind of definition I should have to consider in the first place how people generally used the word ... but my business is not with its proper usage, as established by custom. I should, indeed, be foolish if I tried to use it for something which it did not usually denote: if, for instance, I were to announce that, whenever I used the word 'good', I must be understood to be thinking of that object which is usually denoted by the word 'table'. I shall, therefore, use the world in the sense in which I think it is ordinarily used; but at the same time I am not anxious to discuss whether I am right in thinking it is so used. My business is solely with that object or idea, which I hold, rightly or wrongly, that the word is generally used to stand for. What I want to discover is the nature of that object or idea. (Moore [1903], §6)

The object of analysis, this 'object or idea', is now generally called a concept, just the sort of thing apparently envisioned in Stroud's 'everyday concept of knowledge'.

The analysis, difficult as it may be,[38] is carried out by considering cases, guided by our 'general knowledge of the

---

38. Moore [1903], Preface: 'the work of analysis and distinction is often very difficult: we may often fail to make the necessary discovery, even though we make a definite attempt to do so'.

English language' (Moore [1933/4], p. 191): we propose an analysis, concoct test cases to see if we can find one that satisfies the analysis but doesn't fall under the concept, or vice versa; if we succeed in finding such a counterexample, we amend the analysis; and so on. For example, I might propose 'mother's mother' as an analysis of 'grandmother', then notice the possibility of paternal grandmothers and amend to 'parent's mother'. One especially famous instance of counter-exampling concerns our very own case, the concept of knowledge. Since antiquity, it had been thought that to know something is to believe it, to be justified in believing it, and for it to be true. Then in 1963, Edmund Gettier described a series of cases along these lines: you believe I own a Chevy because you see me driving one to work every day; I do own a Chevy, but the one you've seen me driving to work belongs to my sister (we swap cars sometimes so that she can take advantage of the carpool exemption on my Volt); so you have a justified, true belief, but most people agree that you don't know.[39] This unexpected failure of tradition thinking motivated the contemporary focus on this particular conceptual analysis and inspired a long and so far inconclusive search for an extra condition—beyond justified, true belief—that can withstand counter-exampling.

This new perspective of Moore's, the emphasis on conceptual analysis, marked the birth of what's now known as

---

39. Not everyone. See Weinberg, Nichols, and Stich [2001], pp. 28–31, for some cross-cultural surprises.

'analytic philosophy'. Austin was an unabashed admirer of Moore,[40] and there is, as just noted, a tendency to see Austin as working in this tradition.[41] Nevertheless, two of Austin's early papers mount a strenuous attack on the very idea of a 'concept'. He begins with the traditional argument that runs roughly like this:

> We say '*This* is grey', and '*That* is grey'. . . . How is such a practice possible? . . . Since we use the same single *name* in each case, there must surely be some single identical thing . . . in each case: something of which the name is a name: something, therefore, which is 'common' to all [things] called by that name (Austin [1939], pp. 33–34)[42]

Austin's response is simple:

> But why, if one identical word is used, *must* there be one identical object present which it denotes? Why should it

40. He's quoted as having remarked 'Some people like [Wittgenstein], but Moore is *my* man!' (Grice [1987a], p. 381). Grice doesn't share this high opinion of Moore (ibid.). There's some irony here, as Grice seems more sympathetic than Austin to Moore-like conceptual analysis (though in a linguistic-sounding version perhaps based on meaning (Grice [1958], p. 174)), and to the analytic/synthetic distinction (Grice and Strawson [1956]).

41. Though Moore's explicit distancing of his project from matters of usage should give us pause.

42. Many of Austin's moves in this discussion prefigure those of Quine's famous [1948]. Here is Quine's characterization of the traditional argument: 'There are red houses, red roses, red sunsets. . . . These houses, roses, and sunsets, then, have something in common; and this which they have in common is . . . redness' (pp. 9–10).

not be the whole function of a word to denote many things? (Ibid., p. 38)[43]

We make the mistake of thinking that each word in a meaningful sentence must denote something, then infer 'greyness' from the meaningfulness of 'this is grey'.[44]

Austin also considers the proposal that the concept of 'grey' is really is just the meaning of the word 'grey', which leads to an examination of meanings.[45] He points out that though 'what is the meaning of the word "grey"?' is a perfectly good question when understood as asking 'what-is-the-meaning-of-the-word-"grey"?'—consult a dictionary—it loses its moorings when understood in the philosopher's way as 'what-is-the-meaning-of-the-word-"grey"?'

> At once a crowd of traditional and reassuring answers present themselves: 'a concept', 'an idea', 'an image'. . . . All of which are equally spurious answers to a pseudo-question.

43. Cf. Quine [1948], p. 10: 'One may admit that there are red houses, roses, and sunsets, but deny . . . that they have anything in common. . . . The word 'red' . . . is true of each of sundry individual entities which are red houses, red roses, and red sunsets, but there is not, in addition, any entity whatever . . . which is named by the word . . . "redness" '.

44. Austin [1939], p. 40: given 'the error of taking a single *word* . . . as that which "has meaning" . . . we search for what it denotes'. Cf. Quine [1948], p. 11: it can't be argued 'that [the word] 'red', which we all concur in using, must be regarded as [a name] of a single . . . entity in order [to be] meaningful at all. For we have seen that being a name of something is a much more special feature than being meaningful'.

45. Austin [1939], p. 43. Cf. Quine [1948], p. 11, where Quine's opponent grants that 'red' isn't a name, but then insists that of course it has a meaning, which comes to the same thing, 'or something to much the same purpose in the end'. Considering the source, Quine regards this 'an unusually penetrating speech'.

> How quaint this procedure is, may be seen in the following
> way. Supposing a plain man puzzled, were to ask me 'what
> is the meaning of the word "muggy"?', and I were to answer,
> 'The idea or concept of "mugginess" ... the man would
> stare at me as at an imbecile. (Austin [1940], p. 59)

(Note this early appearance of the commonsensical Plain
Man.) There is more, of course, but Austin concludes that 'the
meaning of "grey"' doesn't describe a thing of any kind.[46]

So Austin would be unlikely to agree with Stroud that
there is a 'concept of knowledge' or a 'meaning of the word
"knowledge"' that could be analyzed and seen to depart from
the ragged but effective contours of our actual use of the word
'know'.[47] In Stroud's retelling, Austin's anti-skeptical strategy
comes to this: observe the linguistic practice; infer some features of the concept (in particular, the more lenient requirement that doesn't include ruling out extraordinary dreaming);
conclude that we do in fact know most of the things we think

---

46. Austin [1940], p. 60: '"the meaning of p" is not a definite description of any entity'.
   Cf. Quine [1948], p. 11, after his opponent's 'unusually penetrating speech': 'the
   only way I know to counter it is by refusing to admit meanings. However, I feel no
   reluctance toward refusing to admit meanings'. Both Austin, in the remainder of
   his [1940], and Quine, in his [1951], go on to debunk the notion that some claims
   are true solely by virtue of the meanings of the terms involved.

47. We might say that Austin takes knowledge to be more like Excuses than like Time
   (recalling the quotations on p. 43 from his [1956], pp. 182, 185): our usage of
   'know' is 'a field where ordinary language is rich and subtle', not one where 'our
   interests are more intellectual . . . than the ordinary'. Kornblith ([2002], pp. 10–
   11, [2007], pp. 46–47) disagrees, taking knowledge to be a natural phenomenon,
   like Time, to be studied empirically. See pp. 218–219 of Lecture III for discussion
   of this idea.

we know. Stroud responds to that anti-skeptical strategy by attacking the inference from linguistic practices to features of the concept. In contrast, I'm suggesting that Austin makes no such inference, that he isn't out to investigate the features of the concept at all, because he doesn't believe in concepts. Rather, he's out to display the ins-and-outs of our use of 'know', the subtle distinctions marked, their effectiveness in a wide range of practical circumstances, and so on. At that point, it becomes clear that requiring that extraordinary dreaming be ruled out, which can't ever be done, would result in a vastly less useful linguistic practice. So Austin isn't claiming that the skeptic would be employing a different concept, the position Stroud is out to rebut; on Austin's view, unlike Stroud's, there are no concepts, the linguistic usage is all there is. Rather, once he's laid out our well-honed and effective practice with the word 'know', Austin can leave us to compare it with a proposed more stringent practice, and we're expected to recognize the obvious: that the actual practice wins hands down. I confess I think he's right here, on all counts.[48]

---

48. One last remark on 'the concept of knowledge'. As the analyses and counterexamples in the contemporary literature become increasingly complex—and they do! (e.g., see footnote 31 of Lecture III)—there's no reason to suppose that even the subtle ins-and-outs of our usage of 'know' will settle the issues raised. See Austin [1940], pp. 67–68: 'Suppose that I live in harmony and friendship for four years with a cat: and then it delivers a philippic. We ask ourselves, perhaps, "Is it a real cat? Or is it *not* a real cat?" "Either it *is*, or it *is not*, but we cannot be sure which." Now actually, that is not so: *neither* . . . fits the facts semantically: each is designed for other situations than this one. . . . With sound instinct, the plain man turns in such cases to Watson and says, "Well now, *what would you* say? . . . How would you *describe* it?" The difficulty is just that: there is *no* short description that is not

But even if we reject the notion of an objective concept of 'knowledge' that our rough-and-ready linguistic practices with 'know' track only imperfectly, there remains Grice's quite legitimate point that some aspects of usage may reflect our conversational norms, not our true standards—this is the surviving core of Stroud's response to Austin. Distinctions along Grice's lines would surely figure in a complete Austinian account of our usage, somewhere in his catalog of 'what we would say when and why'. It would be inappropriate to criticize the careful plane-spotter for claiming to know a plane is an F when he observes it to have features x, y, and z—because the manual says so and he has reason to believe those who wrote the manual are well-informed and operating in good faith, which they are!—but he still doesn't know because he hasn't ruled out its being a G. Similarly, Stroud suggests, criticizing the witness or the chemist for claiming to know when they haven't ruled out extraordinary dreaming might be 'outrageous' because it violates our norms of politeness or fairness, of 'enough is enough'—but not because we actually think they do know.

The moral of this story is supposed to be that our ordinary attributions of knowledge all take place under the sway of practical exigencies; the Plain Man in ordinary life is invariably faced with that rapidly filling bus and well advised to take a good seat, even if it's not the best of all possible seats. And furthermore, the story continues, just as the careful plane-spotter

misleading: the only thing to do ... is to set out the description of the facts at length. Ordinary language breaks down in extraordinary cases ... *words fail us'*. Cf. the example of the Druids in Wilson [2006], pp. 34–37.

comes to see that he doesn't know the plane is an F when he's told about Gs, the Plain Man can be brought to see that he doesn't know there's a chair in front of him when we give him the opportunity to reflect in theoretical style, without any pressures of time or resources or patience or anything else.

But is this true? Is the requirement to rule out extraordinary dreaming actually one that will turn up in the Plain Man's own way of doing things, as soon as it's no longer masked by practical exigencies? Let's imagine the Plain Man placed in this ethereal setting, awarded a leisurely stay at the Institute, given the means to run any check that seems called for, irrespective of time or cost or tedium, and now ask him again about that chair a few feet in front of him in broad daylight. Suppose he now takes all the time he needs to walk around it, touch it, examine or explore it in any way he can think of. What will happen? It seems to me that fairly soon he'll be satisfied and conclude, much as he did before, that there's a chair in front of him. In simple cases like this one, like Descartes observing the fire in his fireplace, it isn't at all clear that any pressure of practical limitations is actually in play. Of course, we recognize that we do sometimes make do with less than conclusive evidence, for various practical reasons, but in simple cases like these, we come to think we know under the best circumstances there are for such things, with the best possible evidence.

The same is sometimes true of the Plain Inquirer, say in the person of our chemist. Suppose she's done a thorough, comprehensive range of tests, checked and double-checked for possible contaminants or equipment malfunctions, suppose she's prevailed upon her colleagues at other labs to replicate her results. Suppose, like the Plain Man, she's been given unlimited time and resources to remove every question mark. At a certain point, she'll be satisfied; much like the Plain Man, she's checked everything she can think of to check. This isn't to say that either of them is guaranteed to be right—we admitted long ago to our fallibility—but it's hard to see that they've jumped to a hasty conclusion under pressure of practical exigencies.

Still, the skeptic might interject, those inquiries aren't *actually* complete, because neither Plain person has ruled out the possibility of extraordinary dreaming, and they should recognize this when pressed. If this challenge is put to the Plain Man, I doubt that he'd suddenly see it as something he should have thought of and ought to have dealt with, even if he only sputters in his attempts to explain why the suggestion strikes him as daft. The Plain Inquirer will do better: she understands the challenge to rule out extraordinary dreaming, along with the Evil Demon and the Brain in a Vat, as a demand that she defend her beliefs without using any of her usual methods for defending beliefs, the very methods she's put so much energy into developing, assessing, and improving; and she doesn't see her failure, or the Plain Man's failure, to produce some special, hitherto unknown variety of extraordinary evidence to undermine the force of the ordinary evidence they both have so ready to hand.

In cases where our evidence is less conclusive than these, Stroud's observation that we exercise different degrees of diligence in different contexts coheres nicely with the thought that we impose different standards, seek different degrees of probability, depending on the circumstances, depending on the stakes—but this by no means implies that we attain no degree of probability at all along the way. The less-than-optimal, but practically acceptable, seat on that rapidly filling bus is still a seat on the bus; imperfect evidence is still evidence even if it isn't perfectly conclusive.

In the end, then, both Plain persons can be brought to recognize that they can't deliver the kind of certainty Descartes was after, or the kind of 'detached' account of their epistemic position in the world that Stroud's skeptic is after, but they still feel entitled to their 'reasonable beliefs'. So in fact I think Stroud's skeptic *hasn't* successfully shown that the requirement to rule out extraordinary dreaming is somehow covertly present in the Plain Man's and the Plain Inquirer's ordinary and scientific methods for finding out about the world.[49] All the same,

49. It isn't entirely clear to me that Stroud, in his later writings, continues to believe that the skeptical challenge arises out of our ordinary methods. There he places his emphasis on an extraordinary, 'philosophical reflection on our knowledge of the world as a whole', whose 'special features . . . make it impossible to rely on the reassuring kinds of answers we find it so easy to give to what sound like similar questions in everyday life' (Stroud [1996], p. 133). Understanding the skeptical challenge this way, as the result of an extraordinary type of inquiry, may imply that certain kinds of anti-skeptical strategies are ineffective (e.g., externalism, see Stroud [1994]), and may also reveal a kind of 'human aspiration . . . to understand ourselves in a certain way' (Stroud [1996], p. 138) that apparently can't be satisfied, but it doesn't by itself cast doubt on the reasonableness of our everyday beliefs.

While I'm at it, let me also admit that the terse outline of the skeptical reasoning in Stroud [1996] puzzles me in another way. We begin with a perceptual belief acquired in optimal circumstances like the meditator's belief about the fire before him; then 'various considerations are introduced to lead us to concede that we would see exactly what we see now even if no fire was there at all' (p. 131). Are these

it's obvious that those most profoundly moved by the skeptical reasoning don't see it merely as a roadblock to certain special projects. It isn't just that we'd like to reconfigure the foundations of science (Descartes), or achieve a special sort of understanding of our epistemic condition (Stroud), and discover that we can't do it. Even if the requirement on extraordinary dreaming doesn't arise directly out of our ordinary methods,

'considerations' the possibility of ordinary dreaming or of extraordinary dreaming? Given that this is supposed to be of a piece with the way, in a courtroom, I can be brought to 'retreat from [my] claim to have seen the accused go through the door to saying that [I] saw a man in a grey hat and coat go through the door, or perhaps only that [I] saw a figure in a grey hat and coat, which . . . could even have been a woman' (p. 131), the dreaming must be ordinary. Sure enough: 'This so far is still a straightforward question that awaits an answer. Take the question of how, given what you see on your television screen, you know that certain events are now occurring in Washington. Or how, given that you see coats and hats moving in the street below, you know that there are people inside them. I think we believe we could give good answers to these questions. We would appeal to many other things we know to explain the connection in these particular cases between what we see and what we claim to know. We know how television works and we know what kinds of things usually carry coats and hats of the kinds we see' (p. 132). What keeps this from being the end of the story? 'But in philosophy we want to understand how *any* knowledge of an independent world is gained . . . So, unlike those everyday cases . . . we cannot appeal to some piece of knowledge we think we have already got about an independent world' (p. 132). According to Stroud, what's happened is 'the special generality we seek in philosophy, combined with . . . the introduction of certain possibilities of error which are not normally raised in everyday life is what . . . makes the question impossible to answer satisfactorily' (p. 133). The puzzle is this: if ordinary dreaming was at issue in the 'various considerations', then this is a perfectly ordinary possibility of error, and the special generality of the philosophical question by itself is what makes the question unanswerable; on the other hand, if extraordinary dreaming was at issue from the start, then the possibility of error was extraordinary, and the question is unanswerable without any special generality. We don't need both extraordinary dreaming and the special philosophical question; one or the other will do.

it's still alleged to block the force of our everyday and scientific evidence, of even what we take to be our 'highly probably opinions'. To get a sense of what's behind this conviction, of why it can seem so vitally important to rule out extraordinary dreaming, it may help to consider a different style of skeptical reasoning. That's the project for the next lecture.

The Argument from Illusion

We've examined the Dream Argument with some care. There's no denying that it packs an intuitive punch, especially for the philosophically susceptible, but at least some of that punch turns out to depend on taking dreaming in its ordinary, everyday sense when it's argued that it must be ruled out, then in an extraordinary sense when it's argued that it can't be ruled out. Stroud maintains that the requirement to rule out extraordinary dreaming is implicit in our ordinary ways of acquiring and assessing beliefs about the world, but at least for now, our Plain Man and our Plain Inquirer remain unconvinced. Stroud claims that our everyday concept of knowledge is more stringent than our ordinary use of the word 'know' would suggest, but this seems to them implausible for a number of reasons. Furthermore, even he's right about that, even if they have no legitimate claim to 'know' about the world, they see in this no reason to conclude that they have no better grounds for believing than for denying their straightforward perceptual claims and the science built upon them.

Descartes insists on ruling out extraordinary dreaming because he's out to uncover a new foundation for science; Stroud's skeptic, because he seeks a 'detached' account of our epistemic condition. Neither of these goals appears to be attainable, but our Plain persons don't see why their failure to reach those goals—to produce evidence that doesn't depend on anything else they think they have good reason to believe about the world—should undermine the force of the ordinary evidence they appeal to in their investigations. Still, it seems unlikely that anyone deeply moved by the Dream Argument will be swayed by the mundane considerations they provide. So we're left suspecting that we haven't yet fully identified the source of the Dream Argument's appeal.

1. THE ARGUMENT

My hope is that we can make progress on this puzzle by turning our attention to a quite different skeptical argument: the so-called Argument from Illusion. For this we leave the 17th-century European continent, where Descartes meditated in France and Holland, and cross the channel to the British Isles and the 18th century. The early modern philosophers in question—John Locke, the Englishman; George Berkeley, the Irishman; and David Hume, the Scot—all set out on a quest in precisely the opposite direction from Descartes's: rather than casting sense experience as a potential source of error, to be set aside in the search of more certain principles, they take sense experience as epistemological bedrock. Locke sounds the call:

> Let us suppose the Mind to be, as we say, white Paper, void of all Characters, without any *Ideas*; How comes it to be furnished? Whence comes it by that vast store which the busy and boundless Fancy of Man has painted on it with an almost endless variety? Whence has it all the *materials* of Reason and Knowledge? To this I answer, in one word, From *experience*: In that, all our Knowledge is founded; and from that it ultimately derives it self. (Locke [1689], II.i.2)

The skeptical threat then arises from the ensuing account of how sense perception works. What makes this especially troubling is that this time the unwelcome skeptical surprise *does* appear to emerge directly out of our ordinary empirical investigation of the world and our place it in.

Hume is particularly explicit about this. In contrast to Descartes, he holds that no science 'can go beyond experience, or establish any principles that are not founded on that authority' (Hume [1739], Intro., ¶10). His book, *A Treatise of Human Nature*, bears the subtitle, *Being an Attempt to Introduce the Experimental Method of Reasoning into Moral Subjects*, where 'moral subjects' are just those connected with people. Of this 'Science of Man', he writes:

> The only solid foundation we can give to this science . . . must be laid on experience and observation. . . . The

essence of mind being equally unknown to us with that of external bodies, it must be equally impossible to form any notion of its powers and qualities otherwise than from careful and exact experiments . . . We must . . . glean up our experiments in this science from a cautious observation of human life, and take them as they appear in the common course of the world, by men's behavior in company, in affairs, and in their pleasures. When experiments of this kind are judiciously collected and compared, we may hope to establish on them a science. (Hume [1748], Intro., ¶¶7, 8, 10)

Though our Plain Inquirer uses more sophisticated empirical methods, this description surely marks the beginnings of the experimental psychology she herself pursues. If it leads inevitably to skepticism, this is a problem she must face squarely.

The Argument from Illusion begins, as the name suggests, by calling attention to the many cases in which things are other than they appear. Most examples fall into three rough categories. The first includes a wide range of familiar cases, mostly quite ordinary workings of the perceptual system, in which the look of a thing depends on perspective, lighting, distance, and so on: a round penny looks oval when viewed from the side, the Plain Man's red chair looks greyish in low light, a square tower looks round from a great distance. The second group is illusions proper, where something is misperceived: a stick, immersed in water, looks bent;[1] things look double when you press your finger against the side of your eye; and of course, our old friends, the Müller-Lyer illusion and the conjuror's Headless Woman.[2] Finally, there are outright hallucinations, under the influence of drugs, in extreme alcoholism, in psychosis.

Some cases are hard to classify. Presumably the familiar water temperature example is an illusion: the subject's right hand is kept in cold water for a time, his left hand in hot water; when both hands are then placed in the same bucket of lukewarm water, it feels warm to the right hand and cold to the left. Perhaps after-images likewise: the subject stares at a red patch, then turns his attention to a white screen and sees there a green patch. Ghosts and mirages are more problematic, as Austin notes ([1962], pp. 24–25): a ghost might be a hallucination, 'something ... conjured up ... by the disordered nervous system of the victim', or it might be an illusion, 'a case of being taken in by shadows ... or reflections, or a trick of the light'. Similarly a mirage might be a hallucination, 'a vision conjured up by the crazed brain of

1. This well-worn example, like many others we'll discuss, appears in the ancient compilation of Sextus Empiricus ([200], I.119), though the stick was originally an oar.
2. In the first lecture, Austin described her as 'a woman against a dark background with her head in a black bag' (Austin [1962], p. 14). The common carnival side show version is actually a woman seated on a small stage, apparently headless, with mental tubes protruding from her neck and connected to complex machinery. The standard patter tells of an innocent young woman beheaded in a horrific accident, then kept alive by heroic scientists using this elaborate apparatus. The tubes apparently emerging from her neck actually house an array of mirrors that reflect the opposite wall of the uniformly colored interior of the tent.

the thirsty and exhausted traveler', or an illusion, 'a case of atmospheric refraction, whereby something below the horizon is made to appear above it'. Delirium tremens apparently come in both varieties: outright hallucinations of snakes or rats, and misperceptions like mistaking benign wallpaper patterns or items in peripheral vision for insects. But however they're classified, obviously examples could be multiplied indefinitely.

Though Locke appeals to considerations of perceptual relativity in passing (Locke [1689], II.viii),[3] the most comprehensive early modern presentation of the Argument from Illusion appears in Berkeley's *Three Dialogues Between Hylas and Philonous* (1713): Berkeley, in the person of Philonous, uses perceptual relativity and illusion to argue poor Hylas to the wall again and again, based on Hylas's innocent belief that we perceive objects and their properties. In the first outing, Hylas has supposed that water has a temperature, which we can perceive by touch, and Philonous deploys the aforementioned bucket of lukewarm water:

> PHILONOUS: Suppose . . . one of your hands hot, and the other cold, and that they are both at once put into the same vessel of water, in an intermediate state; will not the water seem cold to one hand, and warm to the other?
> HYLAS: It will.

3. Commentators disagree on whether Locke uses these considerations to support his position or to illustrate it. See Rickless [1997], Downing [1998] for discussion.

> PHILONOUS: Ought we not therefore by your principles to conclude, it is really both cold and warm at the same time, that is . . . to believe an absurdity?
>
> HYLAS: I confess it seems so. (Berkeley [1713], p. 66; [1948], pp. 178–179)

There is more, but eventually, Hylas succumbs:

> HYLAS: . . . I am content to yield this point, and acknowledge, that heat and cold are only sensations existing in our minds. (Ibid., p. 67; [1948], p. 179)

Though he's given up on heat and cold, and subsequently on tastes, odors, and sounds, Hylas takes the bait again when Philonous brings up color:

> Hylas: . . . Can any thing be plainer, than that we see [colors] on the objects? . . . (Ibid., p. 70; [1948], p. 183)
>
> PHILONOUS: What! are then the beautiful red and purple we see on yonder clouds, really in them? Or do you imagine they have in themselves any other form, than that of a dark mist or vapor? (Ibid., p. 71; [1948], p. 184)

This prompts Hylas to try a different tack:

> HYLAS: I must own, Philonous, those colors are not really in the clouds as they seem to be at this distance. They are only apparent colors. (Ibid.)

Philonous draws the awkward consequences of this dodge—
which then are the real colors? The ones seen close up, the ones
seen through a microscope, under daylight, candlelight, . . . ?—
until Hylas again concedes:

> HYLAS: I own myself entirely satisfied, that they are all
> equally apparent; and that there is no such thing as
> color really inhering in external bodies. (Ibid., p. 73;
> [1948], p. 186)

Similar considerations are applied to size and shape:

> PHILONOUS: . . . [A]s we approach to or recede from an
> object, the visible extension varies, being at one dis-
> tance ten or a hundred times greater than at another.
> Doth it not therefore follow . . . that it is not really
> inherent in the object?
>
> HYLAS: I own I am at a loss what to think.
>
> PHILONOUS: Is it not the very same reasoning to conclude,
> there is no . . . figure [shape] in an object, because to
> one eye it shall seem . . . smooth, and round, when at
> the same time it appears to the other . . . uneven and
> angular? . . . You may make the experiment, by looking
> with one eye bare, and with the other through a micro-
> scope. (Ibid., p. 76; [1948], p. 189)
>
> HYLAS: I know not how to maintain it, and yet I am loth to
> give [it] up! (Ibid.)

I don't know why Philonous doesn't appeal to the penny that looks differently shaped when viewed from different angles—he does, in another place, observe that 'all sensible qualities [of] figure . . . are continually changing upon every alteration in the distance' (ibid., p. 91; [1948], p. 206)—but in any case, once Hylas has drawn a distinction between real and apparent properties, he again has a hard time figuring out which are which.

When this and much more is concluded, Hylas is finally cowed:

> HYLAS: You need say no more on this head. I am free to own,
> if there be no secret error or oversight in our proceedings
> hitherto, that all sensible qualities are . . . to be denied exis-
> tence without the mind. (Ibid, pp. 80–81; [1948], p. 194)

Having been convinced that the features of objects that he perceives are all actually 'in the mind', not 'in the object', he regroups and proposes a reasonable way to retain the notion that he nevertheless perceives the object:

> HYLAS: To speak the truth, Philonous, I think there are two
> kinds of objects, the one perceived immediately, which
> are . . . called *ideas*; the other are real things or external
> objects perceived by the mediation of ideas, which are
> their images and representations. Now I own, ideas do
> not exist without the mind; but the latter sort of objects
> do. I am sorry I did not think of this distinction sooner;

it would probably have cut short your discourse. (Ibid.,
p. 89; [1948], p. 203)

To this point, what's happened is that Hylas has accepted the
intended conclusion of the Argument from Illusion: we immediately perceive only our own ideas. He then moves on to what's
known today as a 'representative theory of perception': we perceive external objects mediately, by means of our ideas. And
since the senses only get us as far as our ideas, the transition from
ideas to external objects must be the work of reason, of inference.
So the proposal is that our beliefs about the world are inferred
from the ideas, the representations, provided by our senses.

Now Hylas and Philonous agreed at the outset of their
debate that the person who turned out to be the most skeptical
would lose. Here, finally, Philonous springs his trap:

> PHILONOUS: I would ... fain know, what arguments you
> can draw from reason for the existence of what you call
> *real things* or *material objects*. ... My aim is ... to learn
> from you, the way to come at the knowledge of *mate-
> rial beings*. Whatever we perceive, is perceived either
> immediately or mediately: by sense, or by reason and
> reflexion. But as you have excluded sense, pray shew
> me what reason you have to believe in their existence;
> or what *medium* you can possible make use of, to prove
> it either to mine or to your own understanding. (Ibid,
> p. 90; [1948], pp. 204–205)

Sadly, at this point Hylas falters:

> HYLAS: To deal ingenuously, Philonous, now [that] I con-
> sider the point, I do not find I can give you any good
> reason for it. (Ibid., pp. 90–91; [1948], p. 205)

Thus Hylas stands accused of skepticism.[4] 'For the present I am, if not entirely convinced, at least silenced' (Ibid., p. 92; [1948], p. 207). By the end of the third dialogue, Philonous has brought him round to Berkeley's own view—that objects are just bundles of ideas—which reinstates his knowledge of them at the cost of their dependence on the mind. But we needn't follow them that far along this path.

In fact, despite the rhetorical force of Philonous's dismembering of poor Hylas—and I've given only the tiniest taste of the relentless barrage—there remains a gap in this version of the Argument from Illusion, a gap Berkeley himself recognized. In the *Treatise Concerning the Principles of Human Knowledge*, published in 1710, three years before the *Dialogues*, he observes:

> It is said that heat and cold are affections only of the mind,
> and not at all patterns of real beings ... for ... the same
> body which appears cold to one hand, seems warm to

---

4. Actually, Philonous drives him further, to the point of denying the very existence of 'sensible things', but the conclusion that we know nothing of them is enough for our purposes.

another. [Similarly, one could] argue that figure and extension are not patterns or resemblances of qualities existing in matter, because to the same eye at different stations, or eyes of a different texture at the same station, they appear various. . . . It must be confessed this method of arguing doth not so much prove that there is no extension or colour in an outward object, as that we do not know by sense which is the true extension or colour of the object. (Berkeley [1710], §§14–15)[5]

The fact that the perceived color or shape of an object changes as we approach it or view it from different angles or under different conditions shows (at best) that not all the experienced properties are true to the real features of the object. It remains possible, as Hylas notes, that one of those experienced properties is real and the rest only apparent; it doesn't follow that all we perceive immediately are our own ideas. This is no help to Hylas in his debate with Philonous because he's again caught by the skeptical problem that he can't tell which is which, but if the Argument from Illusion is to reach its intended conclusion—that we immediately perceive only our own ideas—then this hole must be plugged.

5. Commentators are divided between the view that Berkeley changed his mind about the efficacy of the argument during the period between 1710 and 1713, and the view that he uses the argument in 1713 only as an ad hominem against Hylas. See Harris [1997] for discussion. (For what it's worth, I lean toward the latter view.)

Which brings us to Hume, the figure in our series of early modern philosophers who does finally draw a skeptical conclusion. Because Berkeley has mounted the Argument in such detail as recently as 1713, Hume, writing in 1739, doesn't feel the need to elaborate at length:

> 'Twill . . . be proper to observe a few of those experiments, which convince us, that our perceptions are not possest of any independent existence. (Hume [1739], 1.4.2.45)

He reminds us quickly of perceptual relativity—'the seeming encrease and diminution of objects, according to their distance, [and] of an infinite number of other experiments of the same kind' (ibid.)—but the key new element turns up with his example of an illusion:

> When we press one eye with a finger, we immediately perceive all the objects to become double, and one half of them to be remov'd from their common and natural position. But we do not attribute a [real] existence to both these perceptions, *and as they are both of the same nature*, we clearly perceive, that all our perceptions are dependent on our organs, and the disposition of our nerves and animal spirits . . . from all which we learn, that our sensible perceptions are not possest of any distinct or independent existence. (Ibid., emphasis added)

What Berkeley purportedly misses in 1710 is that all the experiences as the object comes closer or the lighting shifts or whatever—all those experiences are 'of the same nature'. Hume elaborates later:

> Now from like effects we presume like causes. Many of the impressions [Hume's word for sensory ideas] of colour, sound, etc., are confest to be nothing but internal existences, and to arise from causes, which no way resemble them. These impressions are in appearance nothing different from the other impressions of colour, sound, etc. We conclude, therefore, that they are, all of them, deriv'd from a like source. (Ibid., 1.4.4.4)

This causal principle—like effects, like causes—is drawn from a list of general rules that Hume has previously developed for judging what will follow from what; other examples note that causes and effects are 'contiguous in space and time' and that causes come before effects (ibid., 1.3.15.2).[6] Here it's used to argue that if a range of experienced properties are all 'like', then their causes must be 'like', so since some are just ideas in the mind, they must all be just ideas in the mind.

---

6. Those familiar with Hume will recall that he denies there is anything in the world corresponding to the causal relation, that he claims there is only constant conjunction. But this doesn't keep him from formulating empirical generalizations about those constant conjunctions. See Broughton [1983].

Thus Hume's tighter version of the Argument from Illusion—after which the transition to skepticism follows the same path as with Hylas. Hume recognizes that philosophers will, like Hylas, feel inclined to a representative theory of perception:

> Distinguish ... betwixt perception and objects, of which the former are suppos'd to be interrupted, and perishing, and different at every different return; the latter to be uninterrupted, and to preserve a continu'd existence and identity. (Hume [1739], 1.4.2.46)

Poor Hylas can think of no response when Philonous calls for an account of how to reason from the perception (idea) to the thing. Hume explains how the inference would have to go, and why it necessarily fails:

> Perceptions ... present to us by consciousness ... are the first foundation of all our conclusions. The only conclusion we can draw from the existence of one thing to that of another, is by means of the relation of cause and effect, which shows, that there is a connexion betwixt them ... The idea of this relation is deriv'd from past experience ... But as no beings are ever present to the mind but perceptions; it follows that we may observe a ... relation of cause and effect between different perceptions, but can never observe it between perceptions and objects. 'Tis impossible, therefore, that from the existence or any of the qualities

of the former, we can ever form any conclusion concerning the existence of the later. (Ibid., 1.4.2.47)[7]

Some have tried to draw the sting of this conclusion by seeing it as a conflict between, as we may put it, the Plain Man's views and what can be ratified by the philosopher's Reason, in which case Hume could side with the Plain Man.[8] But Hume himself sees the conflict as arising within the Plain Man's views, as a conflict between his confidence in his senses and his commonsense beliefs about cause and effect.[9] This is a

---

7. Students of Hume may suggest that this argument depends on Hume's specific understanding of causation in Part 3 of Book 1 the *Treatise*, as nothing more than constant conjunction. But (as noted in the previous footnote) this doesn't keep Hume from formulating principles about causal relations, and at that point, in Part 3, these could be causal relations between actual billiard balls, etc. Now, in Part 4, he purportedly discovers that all he immediately perceives is ideas of billiard balls, but the possibility remains open that these ideas allow him to mediately perceive actual billiard balls—this is the point under dispute—and that he could, for example, discover constant conjunctions between billiard balls in the vicinity and the tendency of humans to report billiard ball ideas. So the issue is just whether or not a representative theory of perception, however the causal relation is understood, inevitably leads to skepticism. The essential ingredient in Hume's argument is explored in section 4, below.

8. See, e.g., Strawson [1985].

9. See Hume [1739], 1.4.4.15 (emphasis added): 'Thus there is a direct and total opposition betwixt our reason and our senses; *or more properly speaking*, betwixt those conclusions we form from cause and effect, and those that perswade us of the continu'd and independent existence of body'. Also 1.4.7.4: ''Tis this principle, which makes us reason from causes and effects; and 'tis the same principle, which convinces us of the continu'd existence of external objects, when absent from the senses. But tho' these two operations be equally natural and necessary in the human mind, yet in some circumstances they are directly contrary, nor is it possible for us to reason justly and regularly from causes and effects, and at the same time believe the continu'd existence of matter'. For more, see Broughton [2003].

stark problem for Hume, for the Plain Man and for the Plain Inquirer.

So poor Hume, who started out to bring empirical methods to the study of mind, perception, and knowledge, who began, as he says, with 'an implicit faith' in his senses (Hume [1739], 1.4.2.56)—poor Hume ends up

> of quite a contrary sentiment . . . more inclin'd to repose no faith at all in my senses . . . ready to reject all belief and reasoning, and . . . look upon no opinion even as more probable or likely than another. (Hume [1739], 1.4.2.56, 1.4.7.8)

This is the very place that Stroud thinks Descartes has reached, that Berkeley thinks Hylas has reached, but this time, it's Hume himself who reaches it, and he falters:

> The wretched condition, weakness, and disorder of [my] faculties . . . the impossibility of amending or correcting [them], reduces me almost to despair, and makes me resolve to perish on the barren rock, on which I am at present. (Ibid., 1.4.7.1)

> After the most accurate and exact of my reasonings, I can give no reason why I shou'd assent to it. (Ibid., 1.4.7.3)

> I am confounded with all these questions, and begin to fancy myself in the most deplorable condition imaginable,

inviron'd with the deepest darkness, and utterly depriv'd of the use of every member and faculty. (Ibid., 1.4.7.8.)

The only cure Hume finds for this melancholy is distraction: 'I dine, I play a game of back-gammon, I converse, and am merry with my friends' (ibid., 1.4.7.9). In that spirit, he manages to carry on through two more volumes of the *Treatise*, but the shadow of radical skepticism is never truly dispelled.

The Argument from Illusion, on which this disturbing skeptical conclusion is based, reemerges in early 20th-century Britain, for example, in the writings of Bertrand Russell. In *Problems of Philosophy* (1912), he describes how a table 'appears to be different colours from different points of view', notes that

> colour is not something which is inherent in the table, but something depending upon the table and the spectator and the way the light falls on the table . . . (Russell [1912], p. 9)

and concludes that all the observed colors

> have just as good a right to be considered real; and there-fore, to avoid favoritism, we are compelled to deny that, in itself, the table has any one particular color. (Ibid., p. 10)[10]

---

10. Presumably Russell's 'just as good a right' and 'avoiding favoritism' is playing the role of Hume's 'of the same nature' and 'like effect, like cause'.

After running through texture, shape, hardness and more, he reaches the familiar upshot of the Argument:

> Thus it becomes evident that the real table, if there is one, is not the same as what we immediately experience by sight or touch or hearing. (Ibid., p. 11)

And the equally familiar representative theory of perception follows hard upon:

> The real table, if there is one, is not *immediately* known to us at all, but must be an inference from what is immediately known. (Ibid., p. 11)

What's new in the 20th-century context is the disappearance of 'ideas' and 'impressions' and the introduction of the technical term 'sense data' for 'the things immediately known in sensation . . . colours, sounds, smells, hardness, roughness, and so on' (ibid., p. 12).[11] The notion of 'data' builds in the idea that this is the fundamental source of evidence, from which our beliefs about the world are inferred. We're then left with only this data, the skeptic argues, and no way to infer more; we're trapped behind what's poetically called the 'Veil of Perception'.[12]

---

11. Moore also believes in sense data, as becomes clear in the surprising conclusion to his [1925], though it isn't until [1957] that he fully convinces himself that they aren't parts of the surfaces of objects.

12. This term is due to Jonathan Bennett [1971], p. 69: the theory of ideas 'puts the objective world, the world of "real things", beyond our reach on the other side of the veil of perception'.

This new road to the skeptical conclusion takes two steps. First, the Argument from Illusion is deployed to establish that we immediately perceive only ideas or sense data, and from there, that our perception of ordinary objects is mediate—in other words, a representative theory of perception. Second, the skeptical conclusion is derived from the representative theory. Let's examine these one at a time, beginning with the Argument from Illusion.

2. SHORTCOMINGS OF THE ARGUMENT

An early, vigorous attack on Hume's version of the Argument was mounted during his lifetime by his great admirer and fellow Scot, Thomas Reid. Disappointed in the reception of his 1739 *Treatise*, Hume wrote what he took to be a more accessible presentation of his views in his *Enquiry Concerning Human Understanding* of 1748, and this work contains the passage that becomes Reid's focus. According to Hume, if we follow the 'blind and powerful instinct of nature',

> [t]his very table, which we see white, and which we feel hard, is believed to exist, independently of our perception. . . . Our presence bestows not being on it: Our absence does not annihilate it. It preserves its existence uniform and entire, independent of the situation of intelligent beings, who perceive and contemplate it. (Hume [1748], 12.1.8)

But this universal and primary opinion of all men is soon destroyed by the slightest philosophy, which teaches us, that nothing can ever be present to the mind but an image or perception, and that the senses are only the inlets, through which these images are conveyed, without being able to produce any immediate intercourse between the mind and the object. The table, which we see, seems to diminish, as we remove farther from it: But the real table, which exists independently of us, suffers no alteration: It was, therefore, nothing but its image, which was present to the mind. (Ibid., 12.1.9)

Perhaps this is the forerunner to Russell's table! In any case, here we have the familiar theme of perceptual relativity, this time rung on size.

Reid's reply involves a simple distinction between apparent magnitude and real magnitude:[13]

Apparent magnitude is measured by the angle which an object subtends at the eye. Supposing two right lines drawn from the eye to the extremities of the object making an angle, of which the object is the subtense, the apparent magnitude is measured by this angle. (Reid [1785], II.14, p. 181)

The apparent magnitude of the sun, he reports, is about 31" of a degree. In contrast, the real magnitude of the sun is 'many thousand miles' (ibid.). The two are, of course, closely related:

13. Reid attributes this distinction to Berkeley, but it's not clear this is accurate. We'll stick with Reid's notions.

The same individual object, remaining in the same place, and unchanged [in its real magnitude], must necessarily vary in its apparent magnitude, according as the point from which it is seen is more or less distant . . . this is as certain as the principles of geometry. (Ibid.)

With this distinction in hand, Hume's argument collapses:

The argument is this, the table we see seems to diminish as we move farther from it; that is, its apparent magnitude is diminished; but the real table suffers no alteration, to wit, in its real magnitude; therefore it is not the real table we see: I admit both premises in this syllogism, but I deny the conclusion. The syllogism has what the Logicians call two middle terms: Apparent magnitude is the middle term in the first premise; real magnitude in the second. Therefore, according to the rules of logic, the conclusion is not justly drawn from the premises. (Ibid., p. 182)

Logic aside, Reid also appeals to common sense: we can easily demonstrate that the real table

must . . . seem to diminish as we remove farther from it. . . . How then can this apparent diminution be an argument that it is not the real table? When that which must happen to the real table, as we remove farther from it, does actually happen to the table we see, it is absurd to conclude from this, that it is not the real table that we see. (Ibid.)

He goes on to explain how, as 'the real table [is] placed successively at a thousand different distances ... in a thousand different positions', the apparent size and shape are completely predictable, 'by the rules of geometry and perspective' (ibid., p. 183). We see the real table; it looks different at different distances and from different angles, according to laws of perspective that are well understood.

This line of thought no doubt has much to recommend it to the Plain Man—'of course it's the table I see; it looks just as it should from here!'[14]—but the Plain Inquirer might pause to ask about the relationship between the angle subtended at the eye—admittedly a matter of pure geometry and optics—and visual experience, which is after all the subject of the Argument from Illusion. How does the perceptual process work for Reid, if not by generating a representation followed by an inference?[15]

As it happens, both Berkeley and Reid were pivotal figures in the history of vision science. Berkeley insisted that while geometric optics is all very fine, we must also consider the psychology of perception, which he did at length in his influential *New Theory of Vision* (1709). Reid's greatest contribution was to distinguish between sensation and perception. Sensations,

---

14. Cf. Austin ([1962], p. 29) on the bent stick: 'What is even faintly surprising ... in the idea of a stick's being straight but looking bent sometimes? Does anyone suppose that if something is straight, then it jolly well has to *look* straight at all times and in all circumstances?'

15. See Nichols [2007] for a more complete discussion of Reid on perception.

for Reid, are mere feelings, like pains, devoid of any conceptual or representational content:

> When I smell a rose . . . the agreeable odour I feel, considered by itself, without relation to any external object, is a . . . sensation. It . . . may be conceived, without a thought of the rose, or any other object. [It] can be nothing else than it is felt to be. Its very essence consists in its begin felt; when it is not felt, it is not. (Reid [1785], II.16, p. 194)

> Sensation, taken by itself, implies neither the conception nor belief of any external object. (Ibid., p. 199)

Perception, on the other hand, is quite rich:

> If . . . we attend to that act of our mind which we call the perception . . . we shall find in it these three things. *First*, some conception or notion of the object perceived. *Secondly*, A strong and irresistible conviction and belief of its present existence.[16] And, *thirdly*, That this conviction and belief are immediate, and not the effect of reasoning. (Ibid., II.5, p. 96)

---

16. Reid makes two exceptions to the second, the belief clause: for lunatics, who believe things contrary to their senses, and for skeptical philosophers, who don't believe their senses (Reid [1785], II.5, pp. 98, 99). Of the latter, he remarks, 'Perhaps it might be sufficient answer to this to say, that there is nothing so absurd which some Philosophers have not maintained'.

Here the idea-theorist's identification of the pure sensory experience with perception is being rejected: a sensation is far poorer than most conceptions of what an idea would be[17]— explicitly without content, not the basis for any inference—and a perception far richer—including belief in an external object. An alternative to a representative theory is being proposed.

Reid calls our attention to the series of steps in the process of perception:

> First, If the object is not in contact with the organ of sense, there must be some medium which passes between them. Thus, in vision, the rays of light; in hearing, the vibrations of elastic air; in smelling, the effluvia of the body smelled, must pass from the object to the organ; otherwise we have no perception. Secondly, There must be some action or impression upon the organ of sense, either by the immediate application of the object, or by the medium that goes between them. Thirdly, The nerves which go from the brain to the organ, must receive some impression by means of that which was made upon the organ; and, probably, by means of the nerves, some

17. E.g., Berkeley holds that a visual idea includes shape, while Reid's visual sensation is restricted to color. For Reid, the 'visible figure' of a scene is its projection onto 'a hollow sphere, whose centre is in the eye' Reid [1764], VI.7, p. 95), geometrically 'the same figure with that which is projected upon the *tunica retina* in vision' (ibid.). For reasons I don't pretend to fully understand, he insists there is 'no sensation that is appropriated to visible figure, or whose office it is to suggest it' (ibid., VI.8, p. 101).

impression must be made upon the brain. Fourthly, The impression made upon the organ, nerves, and brain, is followed by a sensation. And, last of all, This sensation is followed by the perception of the object. (Reid [1764], VI.21, p. 174)

'Nature carries on' the process from object to brain impression 'without our consciousness or concurrence' (ibid., p. 175). At that point, the ensuing sensation must be felt or it wouldn't exist, but as we've seen, sensations by themselves have no content:

If Nature had given us nothing more than impressions made upon the body, and sensations in our minds corresponding to them, we should in that case have been merely sentient, but not percipient beings. We should never have been able to form a conception of any external object, far less a belief of its existence. (Ibid., p. 176)

Lucky for us, Nature has formed us in such a way that 'the mind passes immediately from the sensation to that conception and belief of the object which we have in perception' (ibid., p. 177).[18] The transition from the one to the other isn't an inference: it's

18. In fact, 'The perceptions we have, might have been immediately connected with the impressions upon our organs, without any intervention of sensations' (Reid [1764], VI.21, p. 176). As remarked in the previous footnote, Reid thinks this is what actually happens in the case of visible figure: it is 'suggested immediately by the material impression upon the organ, of which we are not conscious' (ibid., VI.8, p. 101).

simply 'the immediate effect of my constitution' (ibid., VI.20, p. 168); 'by the constitution of my nature, my belief is . . . irresistibly carried along' (ibid., p. 172).

To summarize the place of conscious and unconscious elements, Reid introduces a helpful metaphor:

> The process of Nature in perception by the senses, may . . . be conceived of as a kind of drama, wherein some things are performed behind the scenes, others are represented to the mind in different scenes, one succeeding the other. The impression made by the object on the organ, . . . as well as the impression made upon the nerves and brain, is performed behind the scenes, and the mind sees nothing of it. But every such impression,[19] by the laws of the drama, is followed by a sensation, which is the first scene exhibited to the mind; and this scene is quickly succeeded by another, which is the perception of the object. (Reid [1764], VI.21, pp. 176–177)

> In this drama, Nature is the actor, we are the spectators. We know nothing of the machinery by means of which every different impression upon the organ, nerves, and brain, exhibits its corresponding sensation; or of the machinery

19. See Reid [1764], VI.8, p. 101: 'one and the same material impression, suggests both colour and visible figure'. So the impression on the retina, nerves and brain is followed by a sensation, the sensation of color, even though there is no sensation of visible figure.

by which each sensation exhibits its corresponding perception. We are inspired with the sensation, and we are inspired by the corresponding perception, by means unknown. (Ibid., p. 177)

In the good pastor's eyes, all this is just the normal working of my constitution, the makeup of which is of course God's doing:

> The Supreme Being intended, that we should have such knowledge of the material objects that surround us, as is necessary in order to our supplying the wants of nature, and avoiding the dangers to which we are constantly exposed; and he has admirably fitted our powers of perception to that purpose. (Reid [1785], II.5, p. 101)

By trusting his senses, Reid has been kept from 'break[ing] my nose against a post that comes in my way', spared from any number of accidents, and set upon a beneficial course, so in the end

> I consider this instinctive belief as one of the best gifts of Nature. I thank the Author of my being who bestowed it upon me. . . . And now I yield to the direction of my senses, not from instinct only, but from confidence and trust in a faithful and beneficent Monitor, grounded upon the experience of his paternal care and goodness. (Reid [1764], VI.20, p. 170)

He compares God's goodness in giving me these mechanisms of perception with the influence of his 'parents and tutors . . . fair and honest people who have wished me well' (ibid.).

So, where the representative theorists see ideas or sense data as the foundation from which our perceptual beliefs are inferred, Reid sees sensations as mere stops on the tightly scheduled causal train from the object to the perceptual belief. If this is right, we might wonder why Nature bothered to bring sensations onto the conscious stage at all; why not just let the machinery chug from the impression to the conscious conception and belief all entirely back stage until the final denouement? Reid has an answer. Sensations can be agreeable (like warmth) or disagreeable (like hunger), for good reason:

> The author of Nature, in the distribution of agreeable and painful feelings, hath wisely and benevolently consulted the good of the human species, and hath even shown us, by the same means, what tenor of conduct we ought to hold. . . . [P]ainful sensations . . . are admonitions to avoid what would hurt us, and agreeable sensations . . . invite us to those actions that are necessary to the preservation of the individual, or of the kind. (Reid [1785], II.16, p. 198)

Of course the Plain Inquirer looking back, sees here—and in those previous remarks about the benefits of perception—a charming theological foreshadowing of evolutionary theorizing. (My personal favorite along these lines is Reid's remark about how clever it was of the Almighty to place the organ of smell inside the nose, where the breath is flowing in and out![20])

Though vision science has come a long way since Reid, he clearly stands as a worthy contributor to the development of the subject. His methods are thoroughly empirical: the *Inquiry* includes chapters on such topics as the inverted image on the retina,[21] the structure of animal eyes,[22] and the causes, effects, and treatment of 'squint' (strabismus or 'cross-eyes').[23] Where

20. Reid [1764], II.1, pp. 25–26: 'All bodies are smelled by means of effluvia which they emit, and which are drawn into the nostrils along with the air . . . there is manifest appearance of design in placing the organ of smell in the inside that canal, through which the air is continually passing in inspiration and expiration'.

21. The puzzle at the time was this: given that the retinal image is inverted, how is it that we see things right side up? In the course of an extended discussion (Reid [1764], VI.11–12), Reid notes that we don't perceive the retinal image (unless the eye is removed from the head 'and duly prepared' (ibid., VI.12, p. 121)); it's just part of the causal pathway to perception. That confusion withdrawn, he's left to observe the regularities that actually exist between what happens at the retina and what we see: 'I know it to be a fact, that, in direct vision, I see every point of the object in the direction of a right line that passeth from the centre of the eye to that point of the object; and I know likewise, from optics, that the ray of light that comes to the centre of my eye, passes on to the retina in that same direction. Here it appears to be a fact, that every point of the object is seen in the direction of a right line passing from the picture of that point on the *retina* through the centre of the eye. . . . this is . . . a law of our constitution' (ibid., VI.12, pp. 122–123).

22. See Reid [1764], VI.14, where he considers, e.g., animals with eyes pointing in opposite directions on either side of the head and animals whose eyes move independently, rather than in parallel like human eyes.

23. See Reid [1764], VI.15–16. Reid details in the abstract how different possible causes of strabismus would dictate different treatments, describes the reports of others and observations of his own on four strabismus patients, then draws some limited conclusions.

Hume drew his dark skeptical consequences from examples like double vision, Reid takes time to investigate the phenomenon, concluding that

> in perfect human eyes, the centres of the two *retinae* correspond with one another . . . and . . . every other point in one *retina*, doth correspond . . . with the point which is similarly situate in the other. . . . So that pictures, upon corresponding points of the two *retinae* present the same appearance to the mind as if they had both fallen upon the same point of one *retina*; and pictures upon points of the two *retinae*, which do not correspond, present to the mind the same apparent distance and position of two objects, as if one of those pictures was carried to the point corresponding to it on the other *retina*. (Reid [1764], VI.14, pp. 136–137)

Though he doesn't mention Hume here, he might have noted that when Hume 'presses one eye with a finger', he displaces the image on one of the two retinas to a noncorresponding location, and the single object before him looks like two. Reid assures us that these correlations hold

> true invariably in all perfect human eyes, as far as I am able to collect from innumerable trials of various kinds made upon my own eyes, and any made by others at my desire. (Ibid., p. 137)

I think this must strike us as more genuinely 'experimental' than Hume's 'experiments' of noting the commonplace that things look smaller when they're further away. In all this, Reid is behaving as we would expect of a clear-headed 18th-century Plain Inquirer.

Taken in rough outline, Reid's description of the visual process remains in place today: light rays from the object to the eye, action on the retina, nerves from the retina to the brain, visual experience and belief. Optics and the physics of light have of course progressed. As workings of the retina were explored, it became clear that even so apparently simple a task as detecting the outlines of an object is a nontrivial task, and a complex theory has been proposed to explain how, for example, object edges are computed from luminance shifts. The purely phenomenal aspect of vision, the way things look to us, has been studied in detail by experimental psychologists, and it turns out to be considerably different from what our casual introspection might suggest: for example, only the very center of the visual field is actually colored. The prevailing approach to vision these days is to regard it as an information-processing system and to try to figure out what tasks evolution has designed it to do, what algorithms it employs to execute those tasks, and what physiological mechanisms manage to implement those algorithms.

So what does the 21st-century Plain Inquirer have to say about the cases so dear to the representative theorist: relativity, illusion, and hallucination? Perceptual relativity is a central topic of contemporary vision theory, under the heading of perceptual constancy: the play of light on our retinas is constantly changing—the shape, size, and color of that well-worn table shift as we move about the room, as the lighting in the room brightens and dims—yet we perceive a largely steady world of mostly rigid objects with often stable and uniform colors. We perceive the same black type on white paper as we carry our book from indoors into the sunlight, despite the fact that the amount of light reflected off the 'black' portions in the sunlight is much greater that the amount reflected off the 'white' portions indoors.[24] We perceive an unchanging chair-shaped object as we walk around the Plain Man's chair, despite the shifting perspectives; we perceive it as uniformly red, despite the patches of shadow here and of direct sunlight there, and of constant size, despite the increase and decrease of the portion of the retina it commands as we move closer or farther away. We can, with effort, attend to the shifting look of things we see, but this is difficult, and we usually do it quite imperfectly.

We imagine, for example, that the look of a scene is more or less the same as its projection on an imaginary screen perpendicular to the line of sight between the eye and the scene. But in fact this isn't right. Suppose, for example, that you look down a long alleyway with parallel walls. Now attend to the pure 'look' of the scene. If we project the two lines where the walls meet the street below onto that perpendicular screen, the result would be two roughly vertical lines in a flat plane, closer together at the top, farther apart at the bottom. But this isn't at all what it looks like: it looks like a three-dimensional scene, with some perspectival contraction into the distance.

24. See Palmer [1999], p. 125.

What it actually looks like is something in between what you perceive it as being—an alleyway with parallel walls—and a simple projection—those two lines in a plane.[25] Just how and why the perceptual system performs in these ways isn't perfectly understood, but promising hypotheses are being proposed, tested, combined, and refined.

Overcoming perceptual relativity by maintaining perceptual constancy is one of the most basic tasks the visual system manages to execute, but these very mechanisms are responsible for some of the familiar optical illusions. For example, if two identical horizontal line segments are placed between two converging vertical lines, the converging lines evoke our alleyway, receding into the distance, so we see the higher of the two horizontals as longer (because it's farther away). The very mechanism that gives us accurate size constancy in ordinary cases leads us astray here. In other illusions, like the bent stick, we're actually lacking a form of constancy: the visual system compensates for changes in illumination, different perspectives and distances, but it doesn't compensate for the refraction of light in water. David Marr, pioneer of the modern information-processing approach to vision science, makes the following illuminating observation:

A straight stick appears bent if it is partly submerged in water . . . usually our perceptual processing does run correctly (it delivers a true description of what is there), but

25. See Hatfield [2009].

although evolution has seen to it that our processing allows for many changes (like inconstant illumination), the perturbation due to the refraction of light by water is not one of them. . . . [A]lthough the example of the bent stick has been discussed since Aristotle, I have seen no philosophical inquiry into the nature of the perceptions of, for instance, a heron, which is a bird that feeds by pecking up fish first seen from above the water surface. For such birds the visual correction might be present. (Marr [1982], p. 30)

Perhaps we're subject to a kind of error the heron isn't, simply because there hasn't been sufficient evolutionary pressure on us to produce the requisite constancy!

Finally, in the case of pure hallucinations, not just illusions generated by misperceiving something, it could be that these aren't primarily a malfunction in the visual system itself: recall the suggestion from last time that the brain activity of dreaming is akin to that of chemically induced psychosis.[26] But perhaps we can leave the Plain Inquirer's investigations at this point. What hasn't turned up in any of this experimenting and theorizing is evidence of a purely sensory idea or sense datum from which a full perceptual belief is inferred. Though there is talk of 'inference' in the perceptual system,[27] it's a more or less metaphorical usage, intended to describe various unconscious processes along the complex causal path from retinal stimulation to

26. Lecture I, p. 24.
27. See, e.g., Hatfield [2002] for discussion.

perception—all 'off-stage' to use Reid's image, all quietly functioning aspects of the human constitution, as installed by the evolutionary descendant of Reid's benevolent creator.

So Reid and the 21st-century Plain Inquirer study the phenomenon of human vision as best they can, along with everything else: both account for perceptual relativity, illusions and hallucinations without appeal to ideas or sense data; neither is led by the evidence to anything like a representative theory of perception. As they see it, the Argument from Illusion breaks down at its first step: yes, the penny looks oval, the stick looks bent, the woman on the conjurer's stage looks headless, but it doesn't follow that we're actually seeing something other than the penny, the stick, and the woman. Even in a case of outright hallucination, the withdrawing alcoholic wrongly believes that he sees snakes or rats or the proverbial pink elephants where in fact there are none, but it doesn't follow from this that he actually sees something else. If the Argument is interrupted here, right at the start, we needn't even examine Hume's move from the claim that we sometimes see an idea or a sense datum to the conclusion that we always see an idea or a sense datum, much less the final inference to the skeptical conclusion.

Still, though I fully agree with Reid and the Plain Inquirer on these points, I don't think we can be satisfied to leave the matter here, because we haven't yet addressed the striking fact that the Argument can seem so very compelling: if the penny looks oval (from an angle), then *something* must be oval, something that I experience; if the red rose looks grey (in low light), then *something* must be grey, something that I perceive. A few years ago, in a graduate seminar of mine, we got to talking about one of those optical illusions of apparent motion; I think it was one with concentric circles that seem to be rotating. A handful of these bright, attentive, analytically minded young students stubbornly insisted that though the printed pattern wasn't moving, *something* was, something in their minds that they perceived. Try as we might, the rest of us were utterly unable to talk them out of this view, to convince them that what they were seeing was the image on the printed page that only looked as if it was moving. This episode no doubt has something to do with my subsequent fascination with the Argument from Illusion.

I'm not sure I fully understand its appeal even now, but at least I'd like to explore a few of the factors that may contribute to the Argument's impact: first, what Austin calls 'a mass of seductive (mainly verbal) fallacies' (Austin [1962], p. 5);[28] second, perhaps some lingering effects of early modern thought; and finally, a programmatic philosophical motivation that can lead us astray. Let's take these up in turn.

3. WHY IS THE ARGUMENT SO APPEALING?

(i) A response from Austin

In his discussion of the 'seductive fallacies', we find Austin employing another distinctive philosophical method (as

---

28. Notice, by the way, that the book is called *Sense and Sensabilia*, written by a fellow named 'Austin'—wink, nudge.

promised last time). The philosophical claim at issue here is the representative theory of perception, which he describes this way:

> We never see or otherwise perceive (or 'sense'), or anyhow we never *directly* perceive or sense, material objects (or material things), but only sense-data (or our own ideas, impressions, sensa, sense-perceptions, percepts, etc.). (Austin [1962], p. 2)

The usual way of combating such a claim would be to argue for its opposite, in this case, to argue that we *do* perceive or directly perceive material objects, but this Austin explicitly declines to do:

> I am *not* . . .—and this is a point to be clear about from the beginning—going to maintain that we ought . . . to embrace . . . the doctrine that we *do* perceive material things (or objects). (Ibid., p. 3)

OK, but given that his focus is on the Argument from Illusion, in its role as support for the representative theory, perhaps his plan is simply to show that one or more of its premises are false or inferential steps invalid. But this, too, is not his primary goal.

The plan, rather, is to 'unpick . . . one by one' that 'mass of . . . fallacies', by tracing their roots

[f]irst, to an obsession with a few particular words, the uses of which are over-simplified, not really understood or carefully studied or correctly described; and second, to an obsession with a few (and nearly always the same) half-studied 'facts'. (Austin [1962], p. 3)

Among these oversimplifications are 'the deeply ingrained worship of tidy-looking dichotomies' and of course a failure to appreciate that 'our ordinary words are much subtler in their uses, and mark many more distinctions, than philosophers have realized' (ibid.). This sort of thing won't directly refute the Argument, but it may rob it of its force, 'an operation which leaves us, in a sense, just where we began'. Still, in the process,

[w]e may hope to learn something positive in the way of a technique for dissolving philosophical worries. (Ibid., p. 5)

This approach has come to be called 'therapeutic philosophy': we don't enter the lists for or against the Argument; we attempt to treat the person under its sway, to remove its hold. This style of philosophizing is often associated with Ludwig Wittgenstein, one of the most influential figures in 20th-century philosophy. We'll see how Wittgenstein wields it next time, but for now our interest is in Austin's version.[29]

29. On some readings of Wittgenstein, he takes all philosophical problems to be illnesses in need of cure (a thought we'll take up in Lecture III). Austin clearly rejects anything so sweeping; the quotation just cited concludes with an important parenthetical caveat: 'a technique for dissolving philosophical worries (*some* kinds of philosophical worry, not the whole of philosophy)'.

To keep track of how Austin's approach works, let's break the Argument down into its steps:

1. There are cases of perceptual relativity, illusion, and hallucination in which things appear other than they are.
2. In such cases, what we directly perceive are not material objects but sense data.
3. The cases in which we perceive sense data are not distinguishable from the rest.
4. We always directly perceive sense data.

The inference from (1) to (2) is called the sense-datum inference. (3) is Hume's contribution that sanctions the generalization to all perceptual experiences in (4). If Reid and the Plain Inquirer are to be believed—and I myself do believe them—the sense-datum inference is mistaken, so we never so much as reach step (2). Austin would agree with this. Again, on the bent stick:

> Well, we are told, in this case you are seeing *something*; and what is this something . . .? But this question is, really, completely mad. The straight part of the stick, the bit not under water . . . don't we see that? And what about the bit *under* water?—we can see that too. We can see, come to that, the water itself. In fact what we see is *a stick partly submerged in water*; and it is particularly extraordinary that this should appear to be called in question—that a question should be raised about *what* we are seeing—since this, after all, is simply the description of the situation with

which we started. It was, that is to say, agreed at the start
that we were looking at a stick . . . part of which was under
water. (Austin [1962], p. 30)

He goes on to say (here I'm paraphrasing from a different example) that we see a straight stick that looks bent, not an immaterial stick 'or an immaterial anything else'. But Austin's focus
isn't on debunking the inference; it's on the question we're now
hoping to address, 'what in this case should seriously tempt us
to say that we do' (ibid.) see an immaterial something else.

To answer this question, Austin begins with a set of observations about the initial set-up of the question, about the
implicit, purportedly commonsensical starting point from
which the Argument begins. The Plain Man agrees, of course,
that he doesn't always see things as they really are, that perception can sometimes go wrong. 'Material object' is then
introduced as a term-of-art for what we perceive when things
go right. Now there's nothing wrong with introducing a term-
of-art, though it's 'often thought to be necessary just because
what we've got already has been misrepresented' (Austin
[1962], p. 63), but if we use new vocabulary or give special
meaning to existing vocabulary, we're bound to do so clearly
and explicitly.[30] In the case of 'material object', all we're given is
a series of well-worn examples—tables, chairs, trees, cats—all

30. Reid ([1785], I.1, p. 38) makes the same point: 'when we have occasion to enlarge
   or restrict the meaning of a common word, or give it more precision than it has in
   common language, the reader ought to have warning of this, otherwise we shall
   impose upon ourselves and upon him'.

'moderate-sized specimens of dry goods' (ibid., p. 8) in Austin's phrase (a phrase that entered the philosophical vocabulary so insidiously that it's often used today without any awareness of its source, usually in form 'medium-sized dry goods'). But does the Plain Man think all he ever perceives are items like these? Don't we perceive shadows, voices, mists?

> There is no *one* kind of thing that we 'perceive' but many *different* kinds, the number being reducible if at all by scientific investigation and not by philosophy: pens are in many ways though not in all ways unlike rainbows, which are in many ways though not in all ways unlike after-images, which in turn are in many ways but not in all ways unlike pictures on the cinema-screen—and so on, without assignable limit. (Austin [1962], p. 4)

Here Austin leaves open the possibility that the Plain Inquirer will find some simpler classification of precisely the kinds of things we perceive (though this seems unlikely); his point is that the Plain Man is in no position to specify a single category of things he perceives.

In fact, Austin suggests that this distortion of common sense slipped by us because 'material object' was 'functioning *already*, from the very beginning, simply as a foil for "sense datum"' (Austin [1962], p. 8). Though 'material object' pretends to be a normal term—you know, things like tables and cats—it's actually given an abnormal use, as the single kind of thing we perceive when things go right, and this abnormal use is attributed to the Plain Man. In this way, an apparently inno-cent piece of purportedly commonsense vocabulary makes it quite natural to introduce a corresponding term for the kind of thing we perceive when things go wrong—and there we are, with sense data. If it weren't for this unstated goal

> it would surely never have occurred to anybody to repre-sent as some single *kind of things* the things which the ordi-nary man says that he 'perceives'. (Austin [1962], p. 8)

This may be an example of what Austin has in mind when he speaks of 'concealed motives' (ibid., p. 5).

This way of parsing the situation involves at least some degree of premeditation on the part of the philosopher present-ing the Argument from Illusion. This might be done from sheer rhetorical craft—'if I introduce a supposedly commonsensical, but actually distorting term, "material object", the introduction of sense data will appear more natural than it is!'—but it might also be done almost unawares, when a philosopher harbors a preconception that's nearly unconscious or that he takes to be so obvious or uncontroversial as to pass largely unnoticed.

Hume seems to fit this second description. One odd thing about his presentation of the Argument from Illusion in Part 4 of the first book of the *Treatise* is that he's already announced the conclusion as early as Part 2:

> 'tis universally allow'd by philosophers, and is beside pretty obvious of itself, that nothing is ever really present with the

mind but its perceptions or impressions and ideas, and that external objects become known to us only by those perceptions they occasion. (Hume [1739], 1.2.6.7)

He refers the reader forward to Part 4, but it's hard not to suspect that he believes the theory first and presents his truncated Argument from Illusion more or less pro forma, having already adopted the conclusion from his immediate forebears.[31] As we've seen, it's not clear how much store Berkeley set by the Argument, and Locke's embrace of a representative theory may well have been rooted in the new corpuscular science of the day. Perhaps this is why Austin remarks that the philosophers 'who have been most adept' at 'working' the Argument from Illusion—he names Berkeley, Hume, and Russell—'have all themselves felt it to be somehow spurious' (Austin [1962], p. 4). But aware or unaware, they've all been 'fully masters of a certain special, happy style of blinkering philosophical English' (ibid.).

Here Austin is most interested in how a prior adherence to the representative theory could have consciously or

---

31. Cf. Stroud [1977], p. 26, speaking of Hume's version of the representative theory: 'This is a precursor of what's come to be called the "sense-datum theory" of perceiving, and it has been held in one form or another by most philosophers since Descartes. Hume gives little or no explicit argument for it, and none at all at the very beginning of the *Treatise* . . . where it would seem to be most needed. The legacy of Descartes, Locke and others made that part of the theory of ideas completely uncontroversial to Hume . . . Hume is not alone in this. There is very little argument [for the theory] in Locke, either, but Berkeley's *Dialogues* provide an almost complete catalogue of the familiar considerations in support of such a view', i.e., the Argument from Illusion.

unconsciously led to unexamined terminological choices that make the Argument from Illusion seem more persuasive than it should, but I think his observations are easily adapted to the case of a previously uncommitted philosopher, coming to the Argument with an open mind. For such a thinker, 'material object' can't be working as a foil for 'sense datum' from the start, because sense data have yet to emerge from the Argument itself. Nevertheless, the advertised culprits—lack of appreciation for the actual use of ordinary words, careless introduction of technical terms, the oversimplification of false dichotomies—could lead to the same unfortunate outcome. For example, this philosopher might erroneously assume that all cases in which things go wrong are of the same type—failing to appreciate the ordinary complexities—and might then imagine a wildly oversimplifying dichotomy between two kinds of cases: those where things go right and those where things go wrong. Perceiving a 'material object' could then be introduced for the first, and the Argument proceed to show that perceiving 'sense data' is what's going on in the second.

Addressed to this confused thinker, Austin's 'unpicking' would include his debunking of one side of this dichotomy—the idea that there is one sort of thing that happens when things go right—which we've already reviewed. It would also call attention to the variety of ways in which things can go wrong:

Even the plainest of men would want to distinguish (a) cases where the *sense-organ* is deranged or abnormal or in some way or other not functioning properly; (b) cases

where the *medium*—or more generally, the conditions—
of perception are in some way abnormal or off-colour; and
(c) cases where the wrong inference is made or a wrong
construction is put on things, e.g., on some sound he
hears. (Of course these cases do not exclude each other.)
And then again there are the quite common cases of mis-
readings, mishearings, Freudian over-sights, etc., which
don't seem to belong properly under any of these head-
ings. That is to say, once again there is no neat and simple
dichotomy between things going right and things going
wrong; things may go wrong, as we really all know quite
well, in lots of *different* ways—which don't have to be, and
must not be assumed to be, classifiable in any general fash-
ion. (Austin [1962], p. 13)

For that matter, it isn't even roughly true that whenever things
go wrong, we're not perceiving a 'material object':

An ordinary man . . . when for instance he knows that the
ship at sea on a clear day is much farther away than it looks,
does [not] conclude that he is not seeing a material thing
(still less that he *is* seeing an immaterial ship). (Ibid., pp. 8–9)

In this way, our open-minded philosopher might be dissuaded
from the 'tidy-looking dichotomy' between cases where things
go right and cases where things go wrong, and thus saved from
the dangerous terminology of 'material objects' and the subsequent slide into 'sense data'.

Notice that the problematic moves we've been examining here actually infect not just the Argument from Illusion, but even the very question the representative theory is designed to answer: what do we perceive? As we enter Austin's sphere of influence, we begin to see that the question itself fails to do justice to the complexities of human perception, and not just the complexities revealed to the Plain Inquirer in her scientific inquiries, but the complexities obvious to the Plain Man himself, complexities embedded in the subtle turns of our use of the terms 'perceive', 'see', 'smell', 'taste', and so on. When ordinary insights like these seep in, when we begin to doubt that we're coming at the study of human perception in the right way when we ask 'what do we perceive?', the Argument from Illusion hasn't been refuted, no premise or inference has been attacked, but perhaps we do begin 'to rid ourselves of such illusions as the argument from illusion' (Austin [1962], p. 4).

Another unsettling Plain Man's observation is that many of the cases typically cited in the Argument aren't actually cases in which things go wrong—an elaboration of Reid's point that Hume's table looks exactly as it ought to look from where he's standing. Austin puts it this way:

The cases . . . in which a plain man might say he was 'deceived by his senses' are not at all common. In particular, he would *not* say this when confronted with ordinary cases of perspective [or] with ordinary mirror-images . . . in fact, when he . . . looks down the long straight road, or at his face in the mirror, he is not, or at least is hardly ever, *deceived* at all. (Austin [1962], p. 12)

On some rare occasion, we might be fooled by a straight object immersed in water, but more commonly, we see the situation for exactly what it is: a straight object immersed in water. So when the first step of the Argument begins by listing cases of perceptual relativity and illusion, there's the suggestion that it's

simply mentioning cases which the plain man already concedes as cases of 'deceptions of the senses'. . . . In fact this is very far indeed from being the case. (Ibid.)

So, in addition to noting that the Argument relies on artificial, overly simplified vocabulary, the open-minded philosopher should now worry that the Argument is starting out on a much weaker note than is implied.

Another characteristically verbal error comes with the introduction of the term 'directly perceive' in the second step—'one of the less conspicuous snakes in the linguistic grass' (Austin [1962], p. 15):

We are given no explanation or definition . . . on the contrary, [the term] is glibly trotted out as if we were all quite familiar with it already. (Austin [1962], p. 19)

We may assume, then, that it's intended in an everyday sense. Austin sets to work on this, noting that the Plain Man might say that he sees something indirectly when he sees it through a periscope or in a mirror. Most often, indirect seeing involves an indirect line of sight, so that seeing through binoculars, for example, isn't so much not 'direct' as not 'with the naked eye'. Though the Argument speaks of 'indirect perception', not just 'indirect seeing', it isn't entirely clear what indirect hearing or touching or smelling would be like. Even many visual cases are unclear, like seeing on television. But none of this is of much help in figuring out what is meant by 'direct' in the Argument:

> The philosophers' use of 'directly perceive', whatever it may be, is not the ordinary, or any familiar, use; for in *that* use it is not only false but simply absurd to say that such objects as pens or cigarettes are never perceived directly. (Ibid., p. 19)

> We have here, in fact, a typical case of a word, which already has a very special use, being gradually stretched, without caution or definition or any limit, until it becomes, first perhaps obscurely metaphorical, but ultimately meaningless. (Ibid., p. 15)

And now the second step of the Argument looks, not exactly false, but surely more than a little odd.[32]

32. To be fair, Philonous does take the time to establish that what's perceived 'directly' (or 'immediately' in his preferred terminology) is perceived without any intermediary or inference (Berkeley [1713], p. 62; [1948], p. 174)—in contrast to my hearing a meow and concluding that my cat is nearby. (Of course the Plain Man would deny that his perception of the chair before him involves any

In contrast to these various linguistic complaints lodged against steps (1) and (2), (3) rests on some 'half-studied "facts"' that purport to underlie the claim that illusions are often indistinguishable from the real thing. Austin, with the backing of the Plain Man, notes

> ... it is simply not true that seeing a bright green after-image against a white wall is exactly like seeing a bright green patch actually on the wall ... or (once again) that seeing a stick refracted in water is exactly like seeing a bent stick. (Austin [1962], p. 49)[33]

Similarly, the purported 'facts' that support the inference from (3) to (4) are also carelessly described:

> If I am told that a lemon is generically different from a piece of soap, do I 'expect' that no piece of soap could look just like a lemon? Why should I? (Ibid., p. 50)[34]

These simple observations don't show that (3) or the inference to (4) can't be repaired, but they might just shake the confidence of those for whom the Argument's line of thought

---

such inference or intermediary.) Austin is critiquing the presentation in Ayer [1940].

33. Recall (from p. 22 of Lecture I) Austin's insistence that dreaming one was presented to the Pope isn't really indistinguishable from being presented to the Pope.

34. Of course this is the weakness of Hume's 'like effect, like cause'.

had previously appeared to flow along inexorably, with nary a twitch or bump.

Like the observation above that most examples of perceptual relativity aren't actually in any way misleading, this part of Austin's case just calls our attention to what the Plain Man clearly understands, to what we all understand until we get caught up in philosophizing; for this we've used Reid's label, 'the philosophy of common sense'. Some of the more linguistic parts of Austin's critique take the form of ordinary language philosophy: calling attention to the subtleties of actual usage and implicitly suggesting it's much more effective than the philosopher's crude substitutes (for example, our actual use of 'perceive' versus the notion that everything we perceive is a 'material object'). And finally, there is the overall therapeutic intent: not to argue that the representative theory is wrong, but to undermine our confidence that the theory, and even the question it addresses, are as straightforward and cogent as we'd imagined.

So, Austin is a man of many methods, and he's used them all to give us some insight into the pitfalls, oversights, confusions, and sleights of hand that can make the Argument from Illusion seem more compelling than it actually is. This accomplishment is recognized beyond the philosophical world, well into the realm of vision science, where Marr writes:

Austin's *Sense and Sensabilia* entertainingly demolishes the argument, apparently favored by earlier philosophers, that since we are sometimes deluded by illusions (for example, the straight stick appears bent if it is partly submerged in water), we see sense-data rather than material things. (Marr [1982], p. 30)[35]

('Deluded', by the way, comes from the presentation of the Argument given by the Oxford philosopher, A. J. Ayer, the presentation that draws most of Austin's fire.[36] Austin argues that the switch from 'illusion' to 'delusion' is another of those unnoticed verbal moves that facilitate the sense-datum inference, because an illusion is a misperception of an ordinary thing and a delusion is separate thing, something wholly made up (see [1962], pp. 22–25).)

(ii) A response from vision science

Still, I think we remain at some distance from understanding why those graduate students of mine were so stubbornly convinced that *something* must be moving when they looked at that optical illusion or that *something* must be bent when the stick looks bent or that *something* must be yellow when we see a yellow after-image on a white wall. Austin's therapeutic treatment isn't likely to help with this because the conviction that *something* must be moving, bent, or yellow appears to arise on its own, quite independently of the Argument from Illusion. For example, we've seen Hume remarking "'tis . . . pretty obvious

35. This immediately precedes his remark about the heron, quoted earlier.
36. Ayer [1940], chapter 1.

of itself', quite apart from what philosophers have argued, that these 'perceptions or impressions and ideas' are what's 'really present with the mind' (Hume [1739], 1.2.6.7). In fact, such support as there is seems to flow in the opposite direction: the brute conviction may well be part of what makes the Argument go down so easily. So where does this conviction come from?

For a sense of this, my suggestion is that we begin with a look at early modern theories of vision. In many ancient theories, the visual system was thought to register information in three-dimensions: our eyes emit some sort of rays or somehow transform the intervening air into an instrument for a species of touch, and in that way, we reach out to the object and register its spatial features as well as its color and the rest. The subject was re-oriented in the medieval period by the great Islamic natural philosopher Ibn al-Haytham or Alhazen (born in Basra in 965 and living mostly in Cairo until his death in 1040). Alhazen criticized these 'extramission' theories and overcame a series of imagined impediments to clear the way for an 'intromission' theory: the rays come from the object to the surface of the crystalline humor (what we now call the lens), where brightness and color are registered at each point; this array of information is transmitted to the faculty of sense. But the array is only two-dimensional, and—as Alhazen and the Plain Man both know—we see in three. Alhazen goes on to describe how the faculty of sense does some judging to reach the full three-dimensional experience and to propose that these judgments, performed over and over, become habitual.[37]

---

37. For more on Alhazen, see Lindberg [1976], chapter 4.

The next great advance came early in the 17th century, when Johannes Kepler realized that the crystalline humor is actually a lens that focuses the incoming rays; Alhazen's point-by-point registration of information at the crystalline is replaced by a truly optical image on the retina.[38] Like Alhazen, Kepler believed that we come to perceive depth by custom and habit. This optical and physiological story was largely adopted by Descartes, but for him, a new question became salient. Once the meditator has adopted the Method of Doubt, once he's elected to distrust his senses, to disbelieve in his body and the world around him, all he has left is what passes in his mind. What does this include? At what point does our conscious visual awareness begin? In Reid's image, when do the machinations of the visual system first come on stage?

When Descartes finished writing the *Meditations*, he sent the manuscript to Mersenne with a request that he solicit reactions, preferably critiques to which he could then respond:

> I will be very glad if people put to me many objections, the strongest they can find, for I hope that the truth will stand out all the better from them. (Descartes [1641a], p. 172; AT III, p. 297)

---

38. The theory of vision drew Kepler's attention after a solar eclipse in 1600: he noticed that during the eclipse, the diameter of the moon measured incorrectly through a pinhole camera; he was led to develop a theory of the radiation of light through a small aperture that explained the phenomenon; he then realized that all astronomical observations were affected not only by the optics of small apertures in the instruments but also by the optics of vision itself, which also takes place, after all, through a small aperture. See Lindberg [1976], pp. 186–188.

Mersenne obliged with six sets of objections from leading intellects of the day, and these, along with Descartes's replies, were published in the first edition in 1641. (A seventh set was included with the second edition in 1642.) In the course of replying to the sixth set, Descartes distinguishes 'three grades of sensory response'.[39] The first of these is the physical stimulation of the sensory organs, 'nothing but the motion of the particles of the organs, and any change of shape and position resulting from this motion'—more or less what Reid will later call an 'impression'. The second grade consists of the resulting 'immediate effects produced in the mind'. This sounds a bit like Reid's 'sensation', but in fact it's an idea, the basis for a judgment which takes place at the third grade of response.

So, for example, in the case of the bent stick,

> Rays of light are reflected off the stick and set up certain movements in the optic nerve and, via the optic nerve, in the brain.

This is the first grade response, 'common to us and the brutes'. ('Brutes' are nonhuman animals.) Startling as it may seem, Descartes believes that only humans, not brutes, have minds, so for us, 'this leads to the second grade, which extends to the mere perception of the colour and light reflected from the stick'. Strictly speaking, this is all we get by vision. At this point, the intellect takes over, and

---

39. This and the remaining quotations in this paragraph and the next come from Descartes [1642], pp. 294–295; AT VII, pp. 436–437.

on the basis of the extension of the colour and its boundaries together with its position in relation to the parts of the brain, I make a rational calculation about the size, shape and distance of the stick.

This is the third grade, though again, it isn't truly sensory. All vision alone gives us is a two-dimensional array of light and color, a mental correlate of the retinal image. Like Alhazen and Kepler, Descartes takes the subsequent judging process to be so habitual and so quick that we don't notice it and imagine that we're simply sensing a three-dimensional world.[40]

The problem here is that for Descartes, the mind is entirely transparent, everything mental is conscious. So presumably we could, in principle, attend to the pure, two-dimensional visual experience and the judging process that leads us beyond it. The visual psychologist William Epstein and the philosopher Gary Hatfield have examined Descartes's writings on this point and were unable to find any appeal to phenomenological or introspective evidence that we have this ability.[41] This leaves Descartes in the awkward position of insisting, on the one hand, that the mind is entirely open to view and, on the other,

---

40. This account from the 'Sixth replies' (Descartes [1642]) is difficult to square with what Descartes says in his more physiological writings ([1632?], and especially [1633?])—so much so that Margaret Wilson, a leading interpreter of Descartes (and Broughton's teacher), concludes: 'the treatments of perception in the *Dioptrics* [Descartes [1632?]] and the Sixth Replies, impressive as they may be in some respects, are far from presenting a coherent and consistent position' (Wilson [1992], p. 37). Hatfield [2015] attempts to square this circle.

41. See Epstein and Hatfield [1979], pp. 374–378, especially pp. 376–377.

that there's a two-dimensional mental image and subsequent act of judging of which we're in fact unaware.

At this point, Hatfield and Epstein make a striking observation: nothing elsewhere in Descartes's system requires him to place the boundary between the purely physiological and the mental where he does. He might have placed it later in the train of visual processing, relegating both the two-dimensional array and the subsequent (unnoticed) 'judging' to pure physiology, so that first entry onto the mental stage would be a three-dimensional image. They tentatively suggest that Descartes may have been unwilling to do this because he preferred to assign comparatively little to the passive workings of our sensory system and more to the active workings of our mental faculties; that way, our perceptual errors could be traced to our own bad judgment rather than our God-given visual apparatus. But this remains speculative.

More than Descartes, Berkeley was a true innovator in the theory of vision, shifting the focus, as noted earlier, from optics and physiology to the psychology of perception. Like Locke, he holds that all our information comes from sensory experience; like Descartes, he holds that everything mental is open to consciousness. Since distance is 'a line directed endwise to the eye' (Berkeley [1709], §2), it isn't present in the purely visual input, so the move from the two-dimensional image to the three-dimensional experience now takes center stage. Furthermore, it must be a thoroughly psychological process, entirely open to introspection, relying only on what's available to sense. This means that geometric inferences[42] of the sort associated with Descartes's 'rational calculations' can't play a role in the perception of distance, because we're unaware of any such computations (ibid., §§4, 6, 12). In their place, Berkeley proposes various consciously accessible cues, like the faintness of distant objects or the number of intervening objects (ibid., §3) or the muscular sensations of directing the eyes (ibid., §§16–20)[43], which can be connected with distance by associative learning.

Despite his acuity on the psychological aspects of perception, the constraints Berkeley places on his account leave him in an uncomfortable position much like Descartes's: he has to explain why we aren't in fact aware of the two-dimensional image or the subsequent associative learning. Much as Hatfield and Epstein suggest that Descartes could have helped himself by locating his mind/body interface differently, George Pitcher, a keen commentator on Berkeley's philosophy, suggests that he, too, could have saved himself a great deal of grief simply by admitting

> what seems obviously true—that visual appearances are three dimensional, that things just do normally look, in a full-blooded sense, to be at various distances from the visual perceiver. (Pitcher [1977], p. 23)

42. E.g., when the two eyes are directed toward a nearby object, the distance to the object can be computed from the angles of the two eyes and the distance between them. See, e.g., Descartes [1632?], p. 106.
43. These muscular sensations serve as contingent distance cues in place of the necessary geometric connections of the previous footnote.

He could have done this, Pitcher argues, while maintaining his key point: that we only immediately perceive ideas. The fact that neither Descartes nor Berkeley availed himself of this avenue may well be an indicator of just how captivating the notion of a two-dimensional mental image really is! The first conscious element in perception could be a three-dimensional image, but somehow that option isn't nearly as attractive.

In retrospect, we see that Reid was in a position to break out of this box. He denies that anything like the retinal image is conveyed up the optic nerve to the brain:

> There is not the least probability, that there is any picture or image of the object either in the optic nerve or brain. The pictures on the *retina* are formed by the rays of light; and . . . their impulse upon the *retina* causes some vibration . . . or . . . motion . . . in the nerve; neither that vibration nor this motion, can resemble the visible object that is presented to the mind. (Reid [1764], VI.12, pp. 120–121)

Here he seems to reject the notion of a two-dimensional mental copy of the retinal image. Furthermore, we've seen that he's perfectly willing to grant the visual system powers that aren't available to consciousness, powers embedded in our constitution.[44] Unfortunately, for all that, he remains under

44. As was his contemporary, Immanuel Kant. Both Kant and Reid were spurred to action by the threat of Hume's skepticism, both found some worldly information lodged in the structures of human cognition not just in raw sensory inputs, but Kant employs the esoteric methods of his transcendental psychology while Reid sticks with the common sense of the Plain Man and the empirical psychology of the Plain Inquirer.

Berkeley's sway and holds that our first spatial perceptions are two-dimensional—his vexed notion of 'visible figure'[45]—and that distance must be learned by association. If it weren't for this holdover, he might have extended his study of the corresponding points on the two retinas and stumbled on stereopsis, the distance information encoded in the disparity between the two distinct images, but as history unfolded, that discovery had to wait for Charles Wheatstone in 1838. The historian Robert Crone [1992] blames the long delay on the Lockean article of faith, embraced by Berkeley but not by Reid, that all we have to go on is conscious sensory experience.

In any case, nowadays stereopsis is one of the most thoroughly and successfully studied topics in the information-processing approach to vision science, as researchers investigate the challenges the visual system faces in computing distance by from retinal disparities, and the algorithms and implementations it employs to meet those challenges. The computations themselves, of course, aren't available to consciousness, and they rely on various 'unconscious assumptions': the system has evolved to exploit a range of statistical regularities in the inputs it receives from the physical world. Finally, of course, experimental psychology hasn't uncovered any phenomenal awareness of a two-dimensional image; as we've noted, even when subjects are asked to report 'how things look' as opposed to how they think things are on the basis of seeing them, the result

45. See footnotes 17–19.

is some sort of intermediate picture, still three-dimensional but not entirely faithful to the real features of the scene. The perennial notion that it's enough for the painter to resist habit and attend to his two-dimensional experience is just another manifestation of the tenacity of this idea. In fact, concocting a flat representation of a solid world is much more difficult than that, which is why painters throughout history have sought the aide of mechanical and optical devices, from Dürer's elaborate drawing frame to Vermeer's likely use of the camera obscura to contemporary uses of photography.[46]

We're left with puzzle of why the two-dimensional mental image has such an enduring hold on the imagination, despite the fact that we aren't actually aware of any such thing. Why do Descartes and Berkeley both elect to locate our conscious awareness where it patently is not, with a mental correlate of the retinal image? To be honest, I see no good reason for this perennial choice apart from the arresting fact that the retinal image is just that, an image. In the entire causal chain from light to object to eye to brain there is exactly one actual image, the one the retina—surely that one image must somehow be reflected in visual experience!

Which brings us back to those recalcitrant graduate students, so keen to endorse the sense-datum inference. The Plain Man, as we've seen, has no reason to flout common sense and happily agrees with the Plain Inquirer and her vision science: what he sees is a straight stick that looks bent, and so on.

46. See the controversial Hockney [2006].

Could it be that the graduate students, exposed to perceptual theory largely in their introductory courses in early modern philosophy, have fallen under the sway of a theoretical account of visual processing that dates to the 17th and 18th centuries, an account friendly to the notion of a mental correlate of the retinal image? If their studies haven't extended to contemporary vision science, perhaps they've been saddled with intuitions about how these things work that have long since been superseded. Even if they weren't exposed to early modern vision science, they were almost certainly steeped in the early modern philosophy that was shaped by that science (maybe not Berkeley [1709], but most likely Berkeley [1710] or [1713]). For that matter, perhaps they too are simply transfixed by the salience of the retinal image, perhaps they too feel the same mysterious draw as Descartes and Berkeley. If this is right, might an introductory course in contemporary vision science free them from the apparent necessity they labor under, allow them to attend, as the Plain Man does, to the actual texture of their own experience? And without the two-dimensional mental image to ground it, might the sense-datum inference not seem quite so inevitable? If Descartes and Berkeley and Reid had access to the experimental psychology and vision science of today,[47] no doubt their philosophizing would take on a very different complexion.

---

47. In one poignant passage, Reid longs for the insights of what we'd call developmental psychology: 'Could we obtain a distinct and full history of all that hath passed in the mind of a child, from the beginning of life and sensation, till it grows up to the use of reason; how its infant faculties began to work, and how they brought forth and ripened all the various notions, opinions, and sentiments, which we find

So I tentatively suggest that the lingering influence, direct or indirect, of outmoded vision science could be responsible for the enduring appeal of the Argument from Illusion, at least partly, for some people, on some occasions.[48] In fact, I think there may be another, less scientific, more philosophical force at work as well, but before we get into that, remembering our interest in methods as well as outcomes, let's pause a moment to reflect on the nature of this discussion of those graduate students. The goal hasn't been to show them that the sense-datum inference is incorrect—that we took to have been accomplished long before—the goal, rather, has been to understand why that move in the Argument continues to persuade them, why, as Austin puts it, the illusion of the Argument from Illusion persists. This is akin to what Austin was up to: an attempt to diagnose the strange attraction of the Argument, with the hope that facing its sources squarely may help defuse it. The difference is that Austin's therapy employs the resources of the

in ourselves when we come to be capable of reflection [introspection]; this would be a treasure of natural history, which would probably give more light into the human faculties, than all the system of philosophers about them since the beginning of the world' (Reid [1764], I.2, p. 15).

48. Another possible influence, which I won't try to elaborate here, comes from the history of fine art. David Hockney [2006] presents impressive and provocative evidence of a dramatic change in the look of paintings around 1420 or 1430—after Giotto, roughly beginning with van Eyck. With a master practitioner's insight, he proposes that this new 'realism' was achieved with the use of optical tools, beginning with mirrors and lenses. These paintings ushered in a new artistic paradigm of faithful representation, a new understanding of truthful depiction that continued to hold sway through the development of more sophisticated devices, from the camera obscura and the camera lucida, up to the chemical camera, projectors, and now the digital camera. The conviction that a photograph is the most accurate and realistic, the truest representation of the world remains strong today. Perhaps this

ordinary language philosopher, while I've been acting largely as a Plain Inquirer.

(iii) A response from epistemology

The final, more philosophical diagnosis begins from the observation that the question 'how do we come to know anything at all about the world?' can easily become entangled with considerations of certainty: Descartes needs certainty to break the grip of sense experience; Stroud thinks the requirement of certainty falls out of the skeptical reasoning.[49] Often enough, epistemologists take the quest for certainty as their motivating goal. Austin draws the connection with sense-data theorizing this way:

> There are sentences which can be identified as intrinsically more adventurous than others, in uttering which we stick our necks out further. If for instance I say 'That's Sirius', I am wrong if, though it is a star, that star is not Sirius; whereas, if I had said only 'That's a star', its not being Sirius would leave me unshaken. Again, if I had said only, 'That looks

leads us to think of our immediate visual experience as akin to a photograph, as a kind of two-dimensional projection. Hockney himself insists, quite persuasively, that this is a mistake: 'Photography is all right if you don't mind looking at the world from the point of view of a paralyzed cyclops—*for a split second*' (quoted in Weschler [1983], p. 6).

49. Perhaps like this: if I have to defend my belief in the Plain Man's chair without appeal to any of the other things I know, then any uncertainty is fatal, because there's nothing to appeal to in order to argue that the failure in question is highly unlikely.

like a star', I could have faced with comparative equanim-
ity the revelation that it isn't a star. And so on. Reflections
of this kind apparently give rise to the idea that there is or
could be a kind of sentence in the utterance of which I take
no chances *at all*, my commitment is absolutely minimal;
so that in principle *nothing* could show that I had made a
mistake, and my remark would be 'incorrigible'. (Austin
[1962], p. 112)

A claim about my current sense datum—I see a slivery patch—
is then imagined to be the end point of this progressive backpedaling, an incorrigible statement. The epistemologist's hope
is that my knowledge of the world can somehow be founded on
this slender basis of certainty.

In this vicinity, one contemporary interpreter of Austin,
Eugen Fischer ([2011], chapter 8), finds an intriguingly
Austinian account of the unmerited appeal of the sense-datum
inference. I'm not sure Fischer's story can be strictly located in
Austin, and I'm not even quite sure I fully understand Fischer's
reading, but however these things may be, what I think Fischer
is saying is undeniably Austinian in character. To see how this
goes, consider the question 'what do you see?' If I'm standing
in front of an abstract painting and I'm asked what I see in the
lower right-hand corner, I might say 'I see a red patch, probably
acrylic paint, given the artist and the period'. Now suppose I'm
standing on a ridge, overlooking a valley, and I'm asked what
I see on the valley floor between two stands of trees. I might
say, 'I see a red patch, probably my car, since that's the direction

of the parking lot'.[50] The first of these, the painting case, is the common use: I'm literally claiming to see an ordinary red patch of paint. The second use is less common: I see something but I'm not sure what it is, so I use this neutral formulation, in terms of how it looks from here. When we hike back to the parking lot, I'm 'quite prepared to say, and quite correct in saying', that the red patch I saw *was* the car, just as I suspected (Austin [1962], p. 92).[51] These two kinds of use coexist without difficulty in ordinary language, with the context easily settling what is intended in any particular case.

Now return to the exchange about Sirius. Ayer imagines the case like this: the subject has been asked to say what he sees and he's responded that he sees a star . . .

> But if he is asked to describe what it is that he's actually seeing, he may say that it is a silvery speck. (Ayer [1940], p. 22)

How are we to understand 'I see a slivery speck' in this case? In ordinary circumstances, it would strike the ordinary English speaker as the less common use, like the car case: the speaker is saying that he sees a silvery speck that he thinks is probably a star though he isn't entirely sure. But the circumstances of this cross-questioning by Ayer aren't ordinary: it's taking place in the context of the progressive backpedaling, the progressive drawing in of one's neck, that Austin has described. In these

---

50. This is Fischer's example ([2011], p. 243).
51. In this passage, Austin is speaking of the 'slivery speck' and the star, but the point is the same.

odd circumstances, the poor harried subject can't be taken in the less common way because that interpretation would take him to be assuming there is *something* that he sees, something he thinks might be a star—his neck is still too far out. So he's taken, instead, to be employing the common use, the paint patch use, except that this time, the actual literal thing that he's seeing must be . . . presto! . . . a silvery sense datum.

Of course we don't explicitly reason this way. What happens is that we're presented with an ordinary English sentence—'I see a silvery patch'—and some ordinary unconscious process of generating its probable meaning simply does its silent job, egged along by the implicit agenda of the person posing the question. Because of the oddity of the context, we're easily led to mistake a less common use for a common use. Fischer calls this an 'unwitting transfer' ([2011], p. 243). If this sort of does happen, it could be another factor in the perennial appeal of the sense-datum inference.

Aside from this intriguing line of thought, one point Austin does make loud and clear is that even statements like 'I see a slivery speck' are not certain, not incorrigible:

> The pursuit of the incorrigible is one of the most venerable bugbears in the history of philosophy. . . . But in fact this ideal goal is completely unattainable. (Austin [1962], pp. 104, 112)

Sticking with colors, he writes:

> Certainly someone might say, 'it looks heliotrope', and then have doubts *either* as to whether 'heliotrope' is right

for the colour this thing looks, *or* (taking another look) as
to whether this thing really looks heliotrope. (Ibid., p. 42)

Ayer is willing to admit that I might make a verbal mistake,[52]
but this ignores Austin's second type of error.

> I may say 'Magenta' wrongly either by a mere slip, hav-
> ing meant to say 'Vermillion'; or because I don't know
> quite what 'magenta' means, what shade of color is called
> *magenta*. . . . (Ibid., p. 113)

Presumably these are the sort of errors Ayer has in mind. But
Austin continues

> . . . or again, because I was unable to, or perhaps just didn't,
> really notice or attend to or properly size up the colour
> before me. Thus, there is always the possibility, not only
> that I may be brought to admit that 'magenta' wasn't the
> right word to pick on for the colour before me, but *also* that
> I may be brought to see, or perhaps remember, that the
> colour before me just wasn't *magenta*. (Ibid.)

The thought is that I might say, and believe, 'I see a silvery
speck'; then be told, 'look again, doesn't it actually look a bit
pinkish tonight?'; and respond, again in good faith, 'well, yes,
now that you mention it, you're right! There is a definite pink

---

52. See Ayer [1940], p. 81.

cast to it'. Perhaps I'm so accustomed to its looking silvery that I didn't at first notice the change. Ayer might insist that I did see a silvery speck the first time and only saw the pinkish hue the second time through power of suggestion, but there seems little justification for this move beyond the hope of protecting the false doctrine of incorrigibility.

The third diagnosis, then, is that when epistemology sets itself the goal of certainty, we begin to think that the ordinary process of successively pulling in one's neck must have an indubitable endpoint, and from there, that if the stick looks bent, I may be wrong about the stick, but there must be something I'm right about. This implicit turn of thought can make the sense-datum inference look inevitable, so another of Austin's therapies is to bring the reader to doubt that anything is truly incorrigible.

4. FROM THE ARGUMENT TO SKEPTICISM

So, where are we? For some time now we've been examining the Argument from Illusion. We've seen that its key step, the sense-datum inference, collapses on fairly straightforward inspection. We turned from there to attempting to account for its enduring appeal, so much stronger than its merits would seem to warrant. Ordinary language analysis revealed the misleading terms in which the Argument is formulated—'material object', 'direct perception'; plain common sense insisted that many if not most of the so-called 'illusions' aren't in fact the least bit illusory; outmoded science, the perennial fascination with the retinal image, and ill-fated philosophical aspirations might all permit the fallacious reasoning to run more smoothly than it should. But we haven't yet considered the second half of the skeptical argument, where the conclusion of the Argument from Illusion—that we only (directly) perceive ideas or sense data—is taken to imply that we can know nothing at all about the world around us. It may seem pointless to bother with this latter argument when its basis has been removed, but I think there is something more to be learned here about the underlying sources of skepticism.

The representative theory of perception, as I've characterized it here, consists of two claims: we immediately perceive ideas or sense data, and we mediately perceive objects by inference from those ideas or sense data. The Argument from Illusion is supposed to establish the first claim, and the second is supposed to follow. Let's grant all this and then ask: does such a representative theory inevitably lead to skepticism?

Since the representative theory isn't true in our world, we need to imagine a world different from ours, in which the human-like creatures are consciously aware of three stages in their perceptual processing: a mental correlate of the retinal image, a stretch of explicit inferring, and a resulting belief about the world. Now suppose the Plain Man in our imaginary world looks down that alleyway between two brick walls. If the real-world Plain Man were to do this, he'd see the scene receding into the distance, and one of the cues his visual system would use is the pattern or 'texture gradient' (as it's called): the many similar bricks on view vary downward in size along the wall; his visual system has evolved to take advantage of various regularities in our world, including the fact that such cases usually involve a bunch of similar items of roughly the same size; it executes an algorithm that relies on this fact to derive the depth of the view.[53] In the imaginary world, we bring this processing on-stage, to use Reid's metaphor. We suppose that the imaginary Plain Man acquires a two-dimensional mental image of a lot of smallish shapes that vary in size in a certain pattern; he believes that this sort of pattern usually arises when items of the same size form a surface that recedes into the distance, so he calls up the appropriate algorithm, calculates the orientation of the walls and the depth of the alleyway, and acquires a belief about the three-dimensional structure of the scene before him.

So, is skepticism inevitable in this world? Well, it seems a Plain Inquirer in this imaginary world could study the perceptual process much as the actual Plain Inquirer does in our world: she begins with her theory of objects, light, and optics; observes people, their surroundings, their introspective reports and perceptual beliefs; explores the physiology of the eye, the optic nerves, the brain; eventually devises, revises, improves an imaginary vision science to describe and explain how this imaginary perceptual system works—and she ends up

53. See Palmer [1999], pp. 234–236.

with a representative theory. Just as the actual Plain Inquirer does in our world, she assesses the strengths of the system, its weaknesses, the kinds of situations is which it's most and least reliable and why—and for that matter she even develops treatments for diseases and abnormalities, eyeglasses, and so on. Why should she be lead to skepticism?

Once again, those of philosophical temperament among you are quietly muttering: "But this imaginary Plain Inquirer is assuming that her own perceptual system is generally reliable! She can't even start her theorizing until she's established that. The imaginary Plain Man, too, is making assumptions to which he's not entitled, assumptions about what the world is like, and after all, the imaginary Plain Inquirer is a Plain Man before she's an Inquirer!" The thought is that both these imaginary figures must begin their investigations of the world armed with nothing but their conscious awareness of the mental correlate of the retinal image and that no good inference can get them from there to knowledge of the world.

But why should they be required to begin there? Here I think Reid again provides the key insight, a point in some ways more fundamental than his important critique of the Argument from Illusion and the representative theory. He considers our several faculties—perception, introspection, memory, reason—and notes that the skeptic is demanding that one of these—perception—be justified by means of another—introspection. Actually, to be more accurate, the skeptic is allowing appeal to reason and memory as well; the odd man out, the one guilty until proven innocent, is perception. But as Reid observes:

> The faculties of [introspection[54]], of memory, of external sense, and of reason, are all equally gifts of Nature. (Reid [1785], VI.4, p. 463)

What grounds could there be for treating them so differently?

The philosopher's exasperated reply is ready-to-hand: "What separates introspection from perception, what makes it more basic, is that I can't be wrong about what I'm experiencing! That's why we insist that perception receive its credentials from introspection." Now there's something odd off the bat about this popular line of thought: if introspection is infallible and perception isn't, then an inference from inner to outer would be welcome, presumably making our perceptual beliefs more dependable than they are on their own, but even without such an inference, it isn't clear why the additional

---

54. Reid writes 'consciousness' here, but in the context (the debate with the skeptic), I think he must mean what he calls 'reflection': 'All men are conscious of the operations of their own minds, at all times, while they are awake; but there are few who reflect on them, or make them objects of thought. ... Although the mind is conscious of its operations, it does not attend to them; its attention is turned solely to external objects, about which those operations are employed. ... I conceive, this is sufficient to shew the difference between consciousness of the operations of our minds, and reflection upon them; and to shew that we may have the former without any degree of the latter' (Reid [1785], I.5, pp. 58–59). Reid counts reflection among our faculties though it's not listed in this particular quotation, and it seems fair to assume it's more or less what I've been calling 'introspection'.

reliability of introspection undercuts the considerable degree of reliability perception enjoys in the first place.

As it happens, we needn't pursue this concern because the more fundamental objection precedes it. We've already seen Austin's rejection of the idea that we can't be wrong about our sense data; Reid expands the critique to all our efforts to observe what's going on in our conscious experience. An entire section of the *Essays* is entitled 'Of the difficulty of attending to the operations of our own minds'. He ticks off a considerable list of impediments: for example, the operations of the mind are constantly shifting, so that it's extremely difficult to maintain and attend to a single mental event;[55] our attention is so habitually drawn to the perceived object that it's difficult to turn it to the perceptual experience;[56] if we do manage to shift our attention to the act of perceiving, we're no longer simply

---

55. See Reid [1785], I.6, p. 60: 'The number and quick succession of the operations of the mind make it difficult to give due attention to them. It is well known, that if a great number of objects be presented in quick succession, even to the eye . . . we retain a confused notion of the whole, and a more confused one of the several parts. . . . No succession can be more quick than that of thought. The mind is busy while we are awake, continually passing from one thought, and one operation, to another. The scene is constantly shifting. Every man will be sensible of this, who tries but for one minute to keep the same thought. . . . Other objects will intrude without being called, and all he can do is to reject these intruders as quickly as possible, and return to his principle object'.

56. See Reid [1785], I.6, p. 60: 'In this exercise, we go contrary to habits which have been early acquired, and confirmed by long unvaried practice. From infancy, we are accustomed to attend to objects of sense, and to them only; and, when sensible objects have got such a strong hold of the attention by confirmed habit, it is not easy to dispossess them. When we grow up, a variety of external objects solicits our attention, excites our curiosity, engages our affections, or touches our passions; and the constant round of employment, about external objects, draws off the mind from attending to itself'.

perceiving, and thus aren't successfully observing, what we set out to observe.[57]

For a concrete example of how wrong we can be about our experience, recall that color vision is poor for objects on the periphery of the visual field (because rods so thoroughly out-number cones outside the center of the retina), but we generally believe that the visual field is uniformly colored throughout: when subjects are asked to fix their focus straight ahead, hold a playing card at arm's length and gradually move it from the side toward the front, they're surprised to discover that they can't tell what color it is until it's nearly straight ahead.[58] Reid discusses another example in connection with double vision. When we attend to a nearby object, those in the background appear double, but

> you may find a man that can say with good conscience, that he never saw things double all his life ... in order to have any reflection ... that he did so, it is necessary that he should look at one object, and at the same time attend to the faint appearance of other objects which are within the field of vision. This is a practice which perhaps he never used, nor attempted. (Reid [1764], VI.13, pp. 134–135)

57. See Reid [1785], I.6, p. 61: 'When the mind is agitated by any passion, as soon as we turn our attention from the objects to the passion itself, the passion subsides or vanishes, and by that means escapes our enquiry. This, indeed, is common to almost every operation of the mind: When it is exerted, we are conscious of it; but then we do not attend to the operation, but to its object. When the mind is drawn off from the object to attend to its own operation, that operation ceases, and escapes our notice'.

58. See Dennett [1991], pp. 53–54. Schwitzgebel [2011], pp. 125–127, gives this example a closer look.

Here Reid reminds us that our introspective skills can be improved with care and practice.

> Of course, the fallibility of introspection doesn't set it apart: In a delirium, or in madness ... memory, imagination and our reasoning powers, are strangely disordered and confounded. (Reid [1785], II.22, p. 251)

Reid concludes that, in fact, all the faculties are on a par:

> We must acknowledge it to be the lot of human nature, that all the human faculties are liable, by accidental causes, to be hurt and unfitted for their natural functions, either wholly or in part: But as this imperfection is common to them all, it gives no ground for accounting any of them fallacious. ... It appears, I think, from what has been said, that there is no more reason to account our senses fallacious, than our reason, our memory, or any other faculty of judging which Nature hath given us. They are all limited and imperfect; but wisely suited to the present condition of man. (Ibid., II.22, pp. 251–252)

Here, of course, the Plain Inquirer agrees.

So a skeptic who demands that perception be ratified on the basis of other faculties, the figure Reid calls a 'semi-sceptic' (Reid [1764], V.7, p. 71), is just misguided:

> Why, Sir, should I believe the faculty of reason more than that of perception; they came both out of the same shop,

and were made by the same artist; and if he puts one piece
of false ware into my hands, what should hinder him from
putting another? (Reid [1764], VI.20, p. 169)

If this is right, and it seems to me that it is, then it's inappropriate to insist that the imaginary Plain Inquirer, or indeed
the actual Plain Inquirer, regard perception as essentially
more suspect than introspection or reason. In the imaginary
world, there's no clear obstacle to her discovering that the
representative theory is true and assessing the reliability of
perception in the usual ways. What leads to skepticism isn't
the representative theory, but the unwarranted privileging of
introspection.

And that isn't all. In fact, the representative theory and
skepticism are independent in both directions: the representative theory doesn't imply skepticism, nor does the failure of representative theory imply the failure of skepticism.
Reid sometimes writes as if refuting representative theory
is enough to refute skepticism, but in those finer moments
quoted above, I think he realizes that it's not: even if my perceptual beliefs come to me immediately, without a mental
intermediary or inference (as Reid would say that they do),
the skeptic will demand that I show why I should take any of
those beliefs to be true. Reid's point still applies: if the skeptic
demands that I do this by showing perception is reliable on
the basis of my introspective evidence alone, then he's unfairly
privileging introspection over perception—and again, it's the
unwarranted preference that's doing the work.

Given that semi-skepticism is the variety that purportedly emerges from the Argument from Illusion, we've now seen that its case for skepticism fails twice over: the Argument doesn't actually establish its conclusion, and even if it did, its conclusion wouldn't support a compelling form of skepticism.

5. BACK TO DREAMING

Given this analysis of the Argument from Illusion, I think we can now better understand what's at issue in the Dream Argument. First, obviously, undercutting semi-skepticism by no means removes the entire skeptical challenge, as Reid clearly acknowledges:

> A thorough and consistent sceptic would never . . . yield this point [that is, embrace semi-skepticism]; and while he holds it, you can never oblige him to yield anything else. . . . To such a sceptic I have nothing to say. (Reid [1764], V.7, p. 71)

> If a Sceptic should build his scepticism upon this foundation, that all our reasoning and judging powers are fallacious in their nature, or should resolve at least to with-hold assent until it be proved that they are not; it would be impossible by argument to beat him out of this strong hold, and he must . . . be left to enjoy his scepticism. (Reid [1785], VI.5, p. 480)

What we have here is the kind of skepticism that the Plain Inquirer took herself to face in the wake of the Dream

Argument: the challenge is to justify her belief in the Plain Man's chair without using any of her carefully honed methods for justifying beliefs, what we called there the 'from scratch' challenge. She, like Reid, admits that she doesn't know how to do this, but she, like Reid, doesn't take the lack of this extraordinary evidence to undercut the force of the ordinary evidence that she does have.

A second point worth noting is that this broader understanding of the skeptical challenge issuing from the Dream Argument isn't always what we find in Stroud. Though extraordinary dreaming and the plight of the plane-spotters do point toward a thorough-going skepticism, in later work, there are passages like this one:[59]

> We come to see our knowledge of an independent world in general as problematic relative to the apparently less problematic knowledge we have of what we perceive. The priority of 'experiential knowledge' over knowledge of objects is in that sense a 'discovery' or outcome which we are led to by applying familiar everyday concepts and distinctions in the course of what is admittedly a special philosophical reflection on our knowledge of the world as a whole. (Stroud [1996], p. 133)

Here Stroud's 'experiential knowledge' (he takes the term from Williams [1996]) isn't necessarily an idea or the

---

59. See also footnote 18 of Lecture I.

two-dimensional mental image of early modern vision science or a sense datum; it could just as well be a report of a perceptual belief: 'It looks to me as if there's a chair in front of me'. And Stroud isn't making any explicit assumption about infallibility, though he does appeal to a procedure like Austin's of drawing in one's neck:

> This kind of procedure . . . is familiar to all of us in every-day life, or in the slightly more specialized example of a cross-examining attorney who gets a witness to retreat from his original claim to have seen the accused go through the door to saying that he saw a man in a grey hat and coat go through the door, or perhaps only that he saw a figure in a grey hat and coat which, for all he saw, could even have been a woman. (Ibid., p. 131)

Though Stroud clearly isn't invoking anything like the Argument from Illusion, the skeptical problem he sees here as arising from the Dream Argument boils down to the impossibility of inferring from inner to outer, of justifying perception on the basis of introspection.

So how does Stroud take this narrower, semi-skeptical version of the problem to emerge from the reasoning of the Dream Argument? In the paper I've just been quoting, he sketches the Argument this way:

> Various considerations are introduced to lead us to concede that we would see exactly what we see now even if no

fire was there at all ['in the fireplace right before us'] ...
I omit the details of this reflection: I assume they are
well enough known for present purposes. (Stroud [1996],
p. 131)

Presumably the considerations in question are the familiar
ones: I might be dreaming (in an extraordinary way) or I might
be systematically deceived by an Evil Demon or mad neuroscientist. This dovetails nicely with the meditator's description of
the Evil Demon:

> I shall think that the sky, the air, the earth, colours, shapes,
> sounds and all external things are merely delusions of
> dreams which he has devised to ensnare my judgment.
> (Descartes [1641], p. 15; AT VII, pp. 22)

Here it's only my perception of 'external things' that's called
into question, so it does seem that Descartes is setting the
semi-skeptical problem. This makes perfect sense for his
purposes: it's the authority of the senses that he needs to
disarm in order to uncover his new scientific truths, so he
has a good reason to aim his challenge there and ignore our
other faculties.[60] But why should the problem be set this

60. Though perceptual knowledge is center stage in the *Mediations*, Descartes does
consider Reason elsewhere. In particular, he takes God's omnipotence to imply
that he could have made the laws of logic any way he liked: he could have made
contradictories true (Descartes [1644], p. 235; AT IV, p. 118); 'he was free to make
it not true that all radii of a circle are equal—just as free as he was not to create the

way by someone who doesn't share Descartes's ulterior motives?

To dramatize the point, notice that the Evil Demon hypothesis needn't take the particular form that it does for Descartes and Stroud. We're all accustomed to focusing on the fact that my perceptual beliefs sometimes don't reflect the actual worldly situation, but our deliberations to this point have revealed that my introspective beliefs about my own conscious states sometimes don't reflect what's actually going on in my mind. Imagine then an Alternative Evil Demon who isn't out to interrupt the connection between my perceptual beliefs and the truth about the external world, but the connection between my introspective beliefs and the truth about of my actual conscious states. Suppose that the world is just as it is, that my visual system works as it should, that my perceptual beliefs are as they should be, and that I act on them appropriately. Of course, all this is entirely contrary to the familiar Evil Demon situation, but our Alternative Evil Demon is more generous on these matters and leaves me in good stead. What the Alternative Evil Demon doesn't allow is reliable introspection: when I pause to reflect, to introspect on my experiences, beliefs, feelings, motivations, goals, and so on, the result is a terrible hodge-podge of falsehoods, rationalizations, and confabulations. For the familiar Evil Demon, the hard part is arranging for a consistent stream

world' (Descartes [1630], p. 25; AT I, p. 152). But God chose to make those laws as he did, and in his benevolence, he also made us so we would take them to be necessary. This casts a new light on anything we prove by our powers of reason, including the inconsistency of a deceiving God. See Frankfurt [1977].

of false experience; for the Alternative Evil Demon, the hard part is maintaining order in these false introspective reports. But both, after all, have 'the utmost power and cunning'!

The semi-skeptical challenge posed by the usual Evil Demon arises when we realize that we can't tell whether he exists or not, so we can't successfully infer from inner to outer. The semi-skeptical challenge posed by the Alternative Evil Demon arises when we realize that we can't tell whether he exists or not, so we can't successfully infer, as we might put it, from inner (my introspective belief about my conscious state) to inner (my actual conscious state). The point of this isn't to enter a new form of semi-skepticism in the epistemological derby—this time casting introspection as the suspect faculty in place of perception—but to illuminate Stroud's claim that the inner to outer semi-skeptical challenge falls out of the reasoning of the Dream Argument. He's right about that, I think, but only because the particular skeptical considerations raised at the key point in that reasoning—embodied in the familiar Evil Demon—are specially designed to raise just that challenge.[61] If we take on board Reid's point that the faculties all stand on equal footing, as I think we should, neither of these semi-skepticisms is well motivated.

The Plain Inquirer saw the Dream Argument differently from the beginning. As soon as she appreciated that extraordinary dreaming was at issue, she assumed that any faculty

61. Williams [1996] would say that Stroud presupposes that 'experiential knowledge' is 'epistemically prior' to knowledge of the world; Stroud [1996] would say this epistemic priority isn't presupposed, but emerges from the skeptical reasoning. I come down in the middle: it isn't presupposed, it emerges, but only when the skeptical hypothesis is carefully structured to produce this outcome.

could be undercut by it: if I can extraordinary dream anything I can experience while waking, then I can extraordinary dream false introspections, false reasonings, and false memories just as I can extraordinary dream false perceptions. We're left, then, with the through-going skeptic and the 'from scratch' challenge. This clarifies the question at issue, but it leaves unanswered the question left open at the end of last time: why does it seem so important to rule out extraordinary dreaming? If we aren't out to found science more firmly (Descartes) or to satisfy a certain philosophical aspiration (Stroud[62]) why should this demand arise at all? And, most centrally, even if it does arise, why should our inability to meet it have anything to do with the efficacy of our everyday evidence? I hope to make some progress on these questions next time.

---

62. As we've just seen, Stroud sometimes sees this narrowly, as the desire for an understanding of our epistemic situation that doesn't rely on any of our ordinary perceptual beliefs, but we're now understanding it as the desire for such an understanding that doesn't rely on the beliefs generated by any of our familiar faculties.

The Cure and Beyond

We've examined two venerable arguments for the radical skeptical conclusion that we know nothing about the world, that we have no more reason to believe the things we do than to believe their denials. The first of these, the Dream Argument, plays in part on a shift from ordinary dreaming to (what we've been calling) extraordinary dreaming. Despite claims to the contrary, the demand that extraordinary dreaming be ruled out hasn't been shown to arise out of our ordinary concept of knowledge, and even if it did, it isn't clear that our purported inability to 'know' would imply that none of our beliefs is more reasonable, more likely, than its opposite. The Argument from Illusion relies on the notoriously invalid sense-datum inference and various other false suppositions that gain undeserved plausibility from a wide range of seductive errors. Furthermore, the inference from its conclusion—the representative theory of perception—to skepticism actually involves an unmotivated semi-skeptical demand that perception be validated on the basis of introspection, an unmotivated demand for an inference from inner to outer, which also turns up in some versions of the Dream Argument.

So our Plain Inquirer is left facing only the pure 'from scratch' challenge—where 'from scratch' doesn't just mean without appeal to anything we think we know about the world by perception, as Stroud sometimes has it, but indeed without appeal to anything we think we know by means of any of our faculties, as Reid puts it, or without appeal to any of our well-honed methods for finding things out, phrased in the Plain Inquirer's terms. She admits, again with Reid, that she can't meet this thorough-going skeptical challenge, that this skeptic must be left 'to enjoy his skepticism'. But they both remain unconvinced that her inability to provide this sort of defense of her belief in the Plain Man's chair in any way undercuts the many ordinary defenses she's perfectly capable of delivering.

Our final question, then, is why some philosophers see the matter so differently, why the possibility of extraordinary dreaming can seem so threatening, why it appears to them so critical that it be ruled out. Why should the unanswerable 'from scratch' challenge have any bearing at all on the status of our ordinary beliefs?

1. MOORE

For reasons that I hope will gradually come clear, I'd like to sneak up on this question by examining one of the most enigmatic and widely discussed of all the profession's copious attempts to respond to the radical skeptic, namely, G. E. Moore's 'Proof on an External World' (Moore [1939]). The Moore at work in this paper is more complex than the Moore that we met in the first lecture, the father of modern analytic philosophy, advocate of conceptual analysis; though the Moore of 'Proof' engages in a fair bit of this, the crucial move has more in common with the forthright judgments of the Plain Man and the philosopher of common sense, familiar to us by now from strains in Reid[1] and Austin. In the end, I hope to suggest that Moore is closer to the Plain Inquirer than might be obvious at first glance, but let's see how this goes.

The paper begins with a quotation from Kant:

> It still remains a scandal to philosophy ... that the existence of things outside of us ... must be accepted merely on *faith*, and that, if anyone thinks good to doubt their existence, we are unable to counter his doubts by any satisfactory proof. (Moore [1939], p. 127)[2]

Moore agrees that this is scandalous, after which he spends the bulk of the paper focused what it takes to be a 'thing outside of

---

1. See footnote 24 of Lecture I.
2. This the Kemp Smith translation. The more recent version by Guyer and Wood has it this way: 'it always remains a scandal of philosophy ... that the existence of things outside us ... should have to be assumed merely **on faith**, and that if it occurs to anyone to doubt it, we should be unable to answer him with a satisfactory proof' (B xxxix). For a brief discussion of Kant's 'proof', see [2011b], pp. 126–134.

us'. He begins with another Kantian notion, 'thing to be met with in space'.[3] For example,

> my body, the bodies of other men, the bodies of animals, plants of all sorts, stones, mountains, the sun, the moon, stars, and planets, houses and other buildings, manufactured articles of all sorts—chairs, tables, pieces of paper, etc. (Ibid., p. 130)

He then remarks that though all of these are things the philosophers call 'material objects', there are things 'to be met with in space' that don't fit that term, like shadows. (We see here an insistence on examples first, a staunch resistance to an overly quick move to the philosopher's generalizing term 'material object', and careful attention to the odd example that most would brush off. We begin to better appreciate Austin's remark that 'Moore is my man'.[4])

Kant tends to equate 'thing to be met with in space' with 'thing presented in space', but now Moore makes a small foray into science, going so far as to quote and cite a psychology manual and a physiology text on the subject of 'negative afterimages'—and even to conduct a few experiments of his own:

---

3. A373. Guyer and Wood have 'things **that are to be encountered in space**'. For those familiar with the Kantian distinction between 'empirical object' and 'thing in itself', this is the former. Moore dismisses the latter (see Moore [1939], p. 139).
4. See footnote 40 of Lecture I.

I took the trouble to cut out of a piece of white paper a four-pointed star, to place it on a black ground, to 'look stead-fastly' at it, and then to turn my eyes to a white sheet of paper: and I did find that I saw a grey patch for some little time [so far the textbook description]—I not only saw a grey patch, but I saw it *on* the white ground, and also this grey patch was of roughly the same shape as the white four-pointed star at which I had 'looked steadfastly' just before—it was also a four-pointed star. I repeated this sim-ple experiment successfully several times. (Moore [1939], p. 131)

(Though this is the only point I know of in Moore's opus where this sort of active experimenting takes place, it is of a piece with Reid's more extensive researches, on his own eyes and the eyes of others.) This after-image, Moore concludes, is clearly 'pre-sented in space',[5] but it isn't 'to be met with in space', because the latter term implies 'that *anyone*, who had been in the room at the time, and who had normal eyesight . . . might have seen . . . it' (ibid., p. 132). Conversely, a thing could be 'to be met with in space' without ever actually having been 'presented' to

---

5. Has Moore made the sense-datum inference here? Shouldn't we just say that with the priming he's given his visual system, the white sheet looks as if it bears a grey pattern of a four-pointed star? May be—Moore is prone to the inference, after all—but it doesn't matter for our purposes. His point is just that showing he experiences after-images wouldn't count as showing there are things to be met with in space, to which we can all agree.

anyone. So Moore leaves 'presented in space' behind and sticks with 'to be met with in space'.

Despite all this, Moore doesn't regard 'to be met with in space' as fully determinate—what about the sky or mirror images?—but he figures there are examples uncontroversial enough—stones, planets, chairs—that showing things of that sort to exist will be enough to show that 'things to be met with in space' exist. He then embarks on an equally detailed, if perhaps a bit trickier discussion of the relations between 'things to be met with in space' and 'things out side of us', which he takes to mean 'things external to our minds'. In ordinary language, Moore notes, to say that I have something 'in mind' is just to say that I'm thinking of it; the thing I'm thinking of may be one of those perfectly ordinary stones or chairs. He hits on the thought that if something is 'in the mind' in the philosopher's sense, then 'I have such and such in mind' implies that I am 'having an experience' (where this naturally gets some parsing, too). So something, say a planet, is 'external to my mind' if 'there is a planet' *doesn't* imply that I'm having an experience. The planet is 'external to our minds' if its existence doesn't imply that any of us are having experiences. He then argues that if such and such is 'to be met with in space', it must also be 'external to our minds'.[6] So, finally, in order to prove that there are 'things outside of us', as Kant thought we

6. One of the more delightful turns in all this is Moore's pause to remark that being 'external to our minds' doesn't strictly imply 'to be met with in space', because the things in dogs' minds are external to ours but not to be met with in space (see Moore [1939], p. 143)!

should, it will be enough to prove that there are things to be met with in space.

What we've done so far seems a fairly good fit for Moore's method of conceptual analysis, as sketched in the first lecture: analyses are proposed, examples examined, analyses modified in light of counterexamples, relations between concepts delineated, and so on. Here I've only given a small taste of these slow and detailed proceedings; at this point, the poor reader is well past the three-quarters point in the paper and near exhaustion. The suspense has built to this climactic moment:

> If I can prove that there exist now both a sheet of paper and a human hand, I shall have proved that there are 'things outside of us'; if I can prove that there exist now both a shoe and sock, I shall have proved there are now 'things outside us'; etc.; and similarly I shall have proved it, if I can prove that there exist now two sheets of paper, or two human hands, or two shoes, or two socks, etc. Obviously, then, there are thousands of different things such that, if, at any time, I can prove any one of them, I shall have proved the existence of things outside us. Cannot I prove any of these things? (Moore [1939], p. 145)

Well, yes he can:

> I can prove now, for instance, that two human hands exist. How? By holding up my two hands, and saying, as I make a

certain gesture with the right hand, 'Here is one hand', and adding, as I make a certain gesture with the left, 'and here is another'. (Ibid., pp. 145–146)

Maybe I should pause a moment for your disbelief to set in. Could Moore really imagine that he has refuted the radical skeptic with this argument?

What little remains of the paper is largely addressed to arguing, back in the slow-but-steady style of the build-up, that the proof is 'rigorous'. He compares it to a proof that there are three misprints on a certain page. How would one prove this?

Surely [I] *could* prove it by taking the book, turning to the page, and pointing to three separate places on it, saying 'There's one misprint here, another here, and another here'. (Moore [1939], p. 147)

Finally, in the concluding three paragraphs, Moore admits he's 'perfectly well aware that in spite of all that I have said, many philosophers will . . . feel that I have not given any satisfactory proof' of the existence of external things (ibid., p. 148), and he tries to figure out what could be bothering them. What they want, of course, is a proof of the premises of the argument, and in fact, not even quite this:

What they really want is not merely a proof of these two propositions, but something like a general statement as to

how *any* propositions of this sort may be proved. (Ibid.,
p. 149)

Here Moore seems to have hit on the 'from scratch' challenge: his opponent is calling all our purported knowledge
of the world into question at once and demanding that the
premises of the argument be defended from there. Now
Moore has our undivided attention; this is what we've been
waiting for! What will he say to the thorough-going skeptical
challenge?

Unfortunately, in these final sentences of the paper, matters
get a bit murky. Still, two points are clear. First, Moore explicitly denies that he can prove 'Here's a hand, and here's another'
because

[i]n order to do it, I should need to prove for one thing, as
Descartes pointed out, that I am not now dreaming. But
how can I prove that I am not? I have, no doubt, conclusive
reasons for asserting that I am not now dreaming; I have
conclusive evidence that I am awake: but that is a very
different thing from being able to prove it. (Moore [1939],
p. 149)

Second, he doesn't think he has to prove this:

Some people . . . think that, if I cannot give such extra
proofs, then the proofs that I have given are not conclusive

proofs at all. And this, I think, is a definite mistake. (Ibid., pp. 149–150)

To unpack the first of these claims, about whether or not he's dreaming, we need to ask if Moore is thinking of ordinary dreaming or extraordinary dreaming. Given that he thinks he has conclusive evidence, it seems he must have in mind ordinary dreaming. But then why can't he give a proof of the familiar ordinary sort?[7]

The answer comes, I think, in his commentary on the second step, on why he doesn't have to prove his premises. It hinges on what he takes his opponent to be asking for. Harkening back to Kant's 'scandal for philosophy', Moore writes:

He means to say, I think, that if I cannot prove that there is a hand here, I must accept it merely as a matter of faith. (Moore [1939], p. 150)

Though this view 'has been very common among philosophers', Moore thinks it 'can ... be shown to be wrong', but there is a catch. It can be shown to be wrong

7. Many contemporary readers of Moore take him to argue from 'I know I have hands (on the basis of my current experience)' to 'I know I'm not dreaming'. If this were so, presumably he *could* tell us what his evidence is. In fact these writers aren't so much concerned with Moore's own views, as they are with an argument inspired by his 'proof'. This is the topic of Appendix B.

> . . . only by the use of premises which are not known to be
> true, unless we do know of the existence of external things.
> (Ibid.)

Though the text doesn't compel this reading, I suggest that what Moore has in mind is this: what the philosopher wants is a proof that Moore knows his premises, a proof that here's a hand and here's another; this would require him to prove that he's not dreaming; he has good evidence that he's not dreaming and thus that his belief in his premises isn't 'merely a matter of faith', but that evidence rests on familiar considerations against ordinary dreaming—various facts about what human dreaming is like—and he can only know those facts if he knows the existence of external things. The philosopher rejects this defense, demanding a 'from scratch' proof, but Moore denies that such a proof is required.

By this route, Moore arrives side by side with the Plain Inquirer: just as she thinks the Plain Man knows there's a chair in front of him (or more cautiously, that the Plain Man's belief is reasonable, highly probable), Moore thinks he knows he has hands; just as she thinks she can show that she, or the Plain Man, isn't dreaming, Moore thinks he can do the same; neither claims to do this without using any of their beliefs or methods for showing things; but neither thinks their failure to produce that sort of extraordinary evidence undermines their ordinary evidence. The Plain Inquirer's route to this shared conclusion takes one slightly different turn along the way—she's faced with extraordinary dreaming, which can only be ruled out 'from scratch'; he's faced with ordinary dreaming but required by the nature of the problem to rule it out 'from scratch'[8]—but this makes no difference in the end.

If this reading of Moore is right, it explains that long, initial discussion in his paper: he's getting the reader accustomed to thinking like a Plain Man—those lists of ordinary objects, commonsense discussions of what's to be met with in space, careful distinction of the ordinary use of 'in the mind' from the philosopher's use, and so on—and even a bit like the Plain Inquirer—when he conducts those experiments with after-images. Having acclimatized us to this approach to philosophical questions, he then waves his hands, presents his proof, and expects us to think, 'What could be wrong with that?!'

This is how I've described the Plain Inquirer: she's just going about her business, investigating the world in her usual meticulous ways, when the skeptic turns up and asks her how she knows she's not dreaming. Well, sure, she had a whole range of reasons for thinking she's not dreaming, from those of the Plain Man to those based on scientific information about the nature of dreaming and waking. What could be wrong with that? The skeptic is placed in the unenviable position of having to convince her that she's required to set aside all her well-honed methods, but why should she do *that*? And even if there's some motivation—as in Descartes or Stroud—why

8. These are the two routes at issue in footnote 49 of Lecture I. There I argue that in Stroud [1996], it appears that he's taking both, which would be overkill.

should her failure on these extraordinary projects also bankrupt her ordinary project?

As I've said, the enigmatic text of the paper certainly doesn't compel this reading of Moore as akin to the Plain Inquirer,[9] but I think there's strong evidence for it in a remarkable set of lecture notes from the academic year 1933–1934. These lectures were delivered just a few years before the appearance of 'Proof on an External World' (1939), on the topic, 'what one is trying to do if one tries to do philosophy' (Moore [1933/4], p. 153)—only a minor variant of our leading question here.

Moore begins, as we might expect, with a discussion of conceptual analysis as one of the things philosophers try to do, [10] but in the third lecture he turns to questions of another kind:

> Questions about reality as a whole, to which one particular answer is 'assumed' or 'presupposed' (in a sense I have yet to define) by *us all* both in ordinary life and in the special sciences. (Moore [1933/4], p. 174)[11]

---

9. One difference between Moore and the Plain Inquirer is that she's quite happy to launch into the science of dreaming or the development of vision theory and no doubt much more, if given the excuse, while Moore's foray into experimentation is quite brief, and I would guess, included mostly just to insinuate that this sort of thing is appropriate in the context. Maybe this is because Moore is an actual person, a philosopher, while the Plain Inquirer is an idealized figure, with equal command of, and interest in, all forms of investigating the world.

10. He also considers other types of analysis, like Russell's theory of descriptions.

11. I take the liberty of spelling out the abbreviations Moore uses in these notes, replacing '&' with 'and', and so on.

As an example, he offers the question of the truth or falsity of this claim:

> Whatever else may be true about the Universe, one thing that's true of it is that there have existed in it in the past very large numbers of material things [or] 'bodies' ... in the sense in which the moon is a body, my body is a body, this desk and blackboard are bodies. (Ibid., p. 175)

In what sense do we 'presuppose' an answer in ordinary life?

> That there have been many bodies is 'presupposed' by us all in ordinary life, in the sense that we have all, in ordinary life, often *observed* facts from which, taken together, it strictly *follows* that there have been many bodies. For instance, I at this moment *observe* that there are a good many human bodies in this room, a good many desks, a good many articles of clothing, a blackboard. And I have very often in the past made similar observations. I've observed in walking down a street that there were a good many houses in it; in looking at a wood that there were a good many trees in it; in looking at a sea-beach that there were a good many pebbles on it. It seems not too much to say that *all* adult human beings have frequently observed facts of this sort: so that in the case of each of us, it follows from many facts that he has observed, taken together, that there have been large numbers of bodies

in the Universe, whatever else may be true of it. (Ibid., p. 176)

Here we have the Plain Man seeing his chair and many other 'bodies' as well. The sense in which science 'presupposes' an answer is slightly different:

They're entailed by *established conclusions* of the sciences. One science, for example, has established that thousands of years ago there existed large numbers of enormous reptiles, ichthyosauri and such like. This is a genuine conclusion of a science and an established one; and from it there follows that there have been many bodies in the Universe. Another science has established that more than thousands of years ago just as now there were millions of stars. This is a genuine conclusion of astronomy; and from it again there follows that there have been many bodies in the universe. (Ibid., p. 177)

Here the Plain Inquirer adds some more rarified cases.

What puzzles Moore is how any *philosophical* posing or answering of the question—are there bodies?—would relate to these ordinary and scientific claims. On the one hand, the claims imply an answer; on the other hand, neither the Plain Man nor the Plain Inquirer tends to put the question in so stark a form. This slender reed brings Moore no solace:

It's true that no special sciences raise these abstract questions themselves; but if the sciences do raise and settle questions from which one particular answer to them *follows*, it seems to me obviously rather a subterfuge to say that in raising them [the philosopher] is raising questions that scientists don't raise. (Moore [1933/4], p. 178)

If the philosopher denies the existence of bodies, 'his answer will *conflict* with, be inconsistent with, the results of the sciences' (ibid.). On the other hand, if the philosopher aims to prove the existence of bodies, 'what's the use of his going over the ground again, and proving again what the scientists have already proved?' (ibid.). It isn't even clear that the question falls in the philosopher's purview, either way:

It's admitted that it's not the business of [the philosopher] to discuss whether millions of stars existed a million years ago: that must be left to astronomy. But if so, how can it be his business to discuss whether it's true that many material things have existed in the Universe or none have? If he comes to the conclusion that they have, he will be merely saying something which the astronomers have already proved; if he says none have, he will be contradicting the astronomers. (Ibid.)

What room can we find for the philosopher even to address the question of the existence of the external world?

One possible opening is the thought that the philosopher will approach the question with a different method from the scientist, but then the question arises whether the method used by the sciences isn't the best and the only proper method for settling such questions. (Moore [1933/34], p. 178)

Moore returns to this stubborn knot again and again in the course of the lectures. In connection with the philosophy of mathematics, he remarks that Russell's discussions of mathematical truth raise

> the same sort of puzzling question as to the relation of philosophy to mathematics, which I said was raised by the fact that philosophers do raise questions to which the sciences imply an answer. Surely it's the business of the mathematicians to decide whether particular mathematical propositions are true? And if so what's the use of the philosopher discussing whether *any* mathematical propositions are true? Suppose he decides they are, can he give better reasons than the mathematicians give? Suppose he decides they aren't. He's contradicting the mathematicians. And aren't they the better judges? (Ibid., p. 185)

An important case for our purposes is the nature of evidence:

> The sciences *do* say not only *p*, ... but there's *good evidence for p*: and it has happened that *p* belongs to a class of propositions with regard to which philosophers have concluded: We *never* have good evidence for a proposition

of that sort. Isn't the fact that the sciences say: Such-and-such *is* good evidence for so-and-so, a reason for saying: It *is* good evidence? (Ibid, p. 189)

Again and again, the same questions. They sound rhetorical, but Moore doesn't make this explicit in any of these passages.

In the final pages of the lectures, Moore finally asks what methods philosophers *have* used to argue for one side or the other on the existence of bodies --and also what methods they *ought* to use. One example of a method actually used to argue that there are no bodies is the attempt to show that 'here is a hand' is actually self-contradictory. This would do the job, so the argument ought to be examined, but Moore doesn't think it survives that examination. On the methods used to support the existence of bodies, Moore cites Descartes, but again he thinks the argument doesn't hold up to scrutiny. In the end, at last, he returns to the theme we've been tracing:

I've insisted the sciences give indirect proofs of [the existence of bodies], by proving that particular material things have existed: I instanced the proof of the existence of Plesiosauri, Ichthyosauri, etc.; and of the existence of millions of stars 10,000 years ago. (Moore [1933/34], p. 194)

Moore's intent is clear: he regards the deliverances of science and common sense as relevant to the question of the existence of the external world and indeed as proving of its existence.

It certainly seems reasonable, then, to see 'Proof of an External World', written only a few years later, as continuing in this same general direction. Rather than say these things directly, Moore simply eases the reader into the point of view of the Plain Man and the Plain Inquirer, then produces one of these proofs. He's switched from the esoteric examples of dinosaurs and stars, realizing that his hands will do just as well, but otherwise the sentiment is the same. And so is his only caveat. Right after the proof just quoted from the lectures, he remarks:

> All scientific proofs of the existence of particular kinds of material things seem to me to assume as premisses the existence of others: the proof of ichthyosauri assumes the existence of fossils; that of stars 10,000 years ago the existence of stars *now*. (Moore [1933/34], p. 194)

Transferred to the context of ordinary hands and the argument of 'Proof', this becomes the observation that he isn't giving a 'from scratch' proof. What's new in 'Proof' is his explicit denial that a 'from scratch' proof is required. So I rest with this reading of Moore's famous argument as of a piece with the Plain Inquirer's reaction to the skeptical challenge: No, I can't produce the extraordinary evidence the 'from scratch' challenge demands, but this doesn't remove the force of my ordinary evidence.

2. WITTGENSTEIN

Despite what strikes me as a wealth of evidence for this reading of Moore, commentators tend to see him as simply failing to grasp the true nature of the skeptical challenge.[12] They take him to rest exclusively with a commonsense perspective, overlooking both Moore's clear affinity with the Plain Inquirer—subtle in 'Proof', explicit in the lectures—and his appreciation for the 'from scratch' challenge in the final pages of 'Proof'. (I can be harsh here, because I once read Moore this way myself!) Conspicuous among such interpreters is Ludwig Wittgenstein, who reads Moore this way in the early passages of his final writings on skepticism. More generally, Wittgenstein favors a particular style of therapeutic philosophy, quite different from Austin's. My hope is that applying this method to Moore—or to Moore as Wittgenstein sees him—might win us some insight into our last lingering question about skepticism: why is it thought that our failure to meet the ambitious 'from scratch' challenge serves to undermine all our ordinary evidence? (Apart from the independent interest of Moore's thought on these matters, this was my ulterior motive for getting 'Proof of an External World' onto the table.)

The Wittgensteinian writings on skepticism that I'm referring to here consist of a set of remarks written between

12. See, e.g., Stroud [1984], chapter III, and (I blush to admit) my [2007], pp. 34–35.

1949, when he discussed Moore's work with Norman Malcolm in Ithaca, New York, and his death in April of 1951. During this final period of activity, Wittgenstein filled a number of notebooks with material on color and psychology as well as epistemology; his literary executors sifted these various remarks by topic and arranged them into three posthumously published volumes, one of which, *On Certainty*, includes the remarks on skepticism. The only work Wittgenstein actually published in his lifetime was the early *Tractatus Logico-Philosophicus* in 1922. His other major work, *Philosophical Investigations*, was finished around 1945 but published posthumously in 1953; it consists of a series of short remarks, running from a single sentence to several paragraphs. Much is now known about the laborious stages of its composition—comprising at least five distinct versions—each marked by seemingly innumerable bouts of writing and rewriting individual remarks, inserting new ones, deleting old ones, ordering and reordering the lot.[13] *On Certainty* consists of a superficially similar series of remarks, but all of it is actually first draft jottings; the selections in the published book have been determined by the editors, not by Wittgenstein himself. This means that though the *Philosophical Investigations* is a notoriously difficult work to interpret, *On Certainty* is even worse: the hapless reader is forced to guess how Wittgenstein might have

13. See Baker and Hacker [2005], pp. 1–6, or Stern [2004], pp. xi–xv.

augmented, selected, revised, and reordered the remarks had he lived long enough to complete the painstaking process of making them into a book. Only the raw materials have come down to us.

Under the circumstances, I propose to begin with a look at Wittgenstein's brand of therapy drawn from the presentation in the *Investigations*, then to sketch in the central application of that method, to the so-called 'rule-following paradox'. This will serve as a template when we venture into *On Certainty*: the goal will be to extract an analogous therapeutic strain from the rough welter of that collection.[14] Obviously the result will be conjectural as a reading of Wittgenstein's views, but I hope it will suggest an answer to the question that's been vexing us here: how does it come to seem so crucial to provide that extraordinary brand of evidence, to rule out extraordinary dreaming?!

So, first a look at Wittgenstein's distinctive brand of therapy. For starters, he's emphatic about the role of philosophy:

> Philosophy . . . can . . . only describe. . . . It leaves everything as it is. (*PI* §124)

---

14. There are those who insist that Wittgenstein left therapy behind in his late writings, especially in *On Certainty*. See, e.g., Moyal-Sharrock [2004], p. 5: Wittgenstein 'somehow lost interest in the therapeutic enterprise in his last years', or Stroll [1994], p. 7: in *On Certainty*, 'Wittgenstein is himself caught up in relatively straightforward, classical philosophical concerns about the nature of certainty and its relationship to human knowledge'. Rogers [2011] makes a compelling case against these claims.

> Philosophy just puts everything before us, and neither explains nor deduces anything.—Since everything lies open to view, there is nothing to explain. (*PI* §126)

It isn't the job of philosophy to present and defend original theories:

> If someone were to advance *theses* in philosophy, it would never be possible to debate them, because everyone would agree to them. (*PI* §128)
>
> We may not advance any kind of theory. There must not be anything hypothetical in our considerations. All *explanation* must disappear, and description alone must take its place. (*PI* §109)

Furthermore, these descriptions must stick to the ordinary:

> Here it is difficult to keep our heads above water, as it were, to see that we must stick to matters of everyday thought, and not to get on the wrong track where it seems that we have to describe extreme subtleties, which again we are quite unable to describe with the means at our disposal. We feel as if we had to repair a torn spider's web with our fingers. (*PI* §106)

Of course many philosophers would say that it's precisely the difficulty of the task that makes it so challenging, so fascinating—and so frustrating, too!

This is where the diagnosis and treatment come in. The trouble is that's easy to get caught up somehow and lose sight of the kinds of considerations that might actually provide answers to our pressing questions:

> The aspects of things that are most important for us are hidden because of their simplicity and familiarity. (One is unable to notice something—because it is always before one's eyes.) The real foundations of their inquiry do not strike people at all. (*PI* §129)

This blindness to the obvious answers is the disease. The treatment, then, is to figure out what's causing it:

> If I am inclined to suppose that a mouse comes into being by spontaneous generation out of grey rags and dust, it's a good idea to examine those rags very closely to see how a mouse could have hidden in them, how it could have got there, and so on. But if I am convinced that a mouse cannot come into being from these things, then this investigation will perhaps be superfluous.
>
> But what it is in philosophy that resists such an examination of details, we have yet to come to understand. (*PI* §52)

The cause of this resistance will vary from case to case, as will the relevant ordinary details:

There is not a single philosophical method, though there are indeed methods, different therapies, as it were. (*PI* §133d)

But in each case, the goal is to make 'the philosophical problems . . . *completely* disappear', so that we can 'break off philosophizing' (*PI* §133).

In the central argument of *Philosophical Investigations*, Wittgenstein applies this approach is to the famous rule-following problem. Suppose we've taught a student how to compute 'add-2', testing him extensively on examples smaller than 1000, but then, when we ask him to add-2 to 1000, he responds with 1004. We know this isn't the right answer, that 1002 is, but the rule-following skeptic challenges us to explain what it is that makes 1002 correct and 1004 incorrect. A wide range of proposals are offered and rejected, including the straightforward idea that we intended 'add-2' in a certain way when we taught it to him, that we meant something specific by it, and that he just missed it:

'The right step is the one that is in accordance with the order—as it was *meant*.'—So when you gave the order '+2', you meant that he was to write 1002 after 1000—and did you then also mean that he should write 1868 after 1866, and 100036 after 100034, and so on—an infinite number of such sentences?—'No; what I meant was, that he should write the next but one number after *every* number that he wrote; and from this, stage by stage, all those sentences follow.'—But this is just what is in question: what, at any stage, does follow from that sentence. (*PI* §186)***

'But I already knew, at the time when I gave the order, that he should write 1002 after 1000'.—Certainly; and you may even say you *meant* it then; only you shouldn't let yourself be misled . . . For you don't mean that you thought of the step from 1000 to 1002 at the time—and even if you did think of this step, still, you didn't think of other ones. (*PI* §187)***

Your idea was that this *meaning the order* had in its own way already taken all those steps: that in meaning it, your mind, as it were, flew ahead and took all the steps before you physically arrived at this or that one . . . it seemed as if they were in some *unique* way predetermined, anticipated—in the way that only meaning something could anticipate reality. (*PI* §188)

When we recognize that we don't, can't, actually grasp or intend an infinite number of cases all at once, we're led to produce some sort of new rule instead. 'The next but one number' is only the first of a long series Wittgenstein's instructor tries, from explicit formulas to mental images or paradigms, but if the student can misunderstand our original teachings, he can just as easily misunderstand all these as well.

And it isn't just that we can't convey our own perfectly determinate meaning to the student; under the skeptic's questioning, we find that we ourselves have nothing more than the very kinds of examples and explanations we can give to him.[15] The upshot of all this is what Wittgenstein calls a paradox:

> No course of action could be determined by a rule, because every course of action can be brought into accord with the rule . . . if every course of action can be brought into accord with the rule, then it can also be brought into conflict with it. And so there would be neither accord nor conflict here. (*PI* §201)

This is the conclusion of the rule-following skeptic: nothing justifies our claim that 1002 is right and 1004 is wrong; there is no fact of the matter about this.

Now the key to reading the *Investigations* is that the conversation involves a number of voices, as we've already seen in this debate between the instructor and the skeptic. Another of these voices, isolated most famously by the influential Princeton philosopher, Saul Kripke, presents what Kripke calls a skeptical solution to the paradox.[16] A straight solution would defeat the skeptic directly, would isolate the fact that makes 1002 correct and our belief to that effect justified. Kripke's voice admits that this can't be done. A skeptical solution goes on from there to

---

15. See *PI* §210: 'every explanation which I can give myself I give to him too'.
16. See Kripke [1982]. Some features of Kripke's reading are anticipated in Fogelin [1976] (see Fogelin [1987], pp. 241–246, for a comparative analysis).

argue that our practice of saying that 1002 is correct is some-how legitimate despite it's not answering to any fact of the matter. Since external world skepticism, not rule-following skepticism, is our central topic here, I won't try to summarize how this goes, but there's no doubting both the skeptical para-dox and the skeptical solution are controversial philosophical theses. Kripke dismisses Wittgenstein's claim to renounce this sort of theorizing, to 'leave everything as it is' as a perhaps dis-ingenuous 'caginess' (Kripke [1982], p. 70), but the goal here is to distill a therapeutic model, so I'll take Wittgenstein at his word on this.

The therapeutic model I have in mind takes the voice Kripke identifies as Wittgenstein's to be, in actuality, just another of the parties to the debate. One of our leading scholars and inter-preters of Wittgenstein, David Stern, describes two general types of voices found in various places in Wittgenstein's writ-ings: the voice of temptation and the voice of correctness.[17] In the rule-following case, the voice of temptation is the instruc-tor who thinks that there's a fact of the matter about what she meant when she taught the student 'add-2', that this justifies her claim that 1002, not 1004, comes after 1000 in that series; and she goes on to offer various theoretical proposals to back up these claims. She's the one beset by the rule-following skeptic, who demolishes each of her ideas in turn. From these sham-bles arises the voice of correctness, who accepts the skeptic's

17. See Stern [2004].

demolition of the voice of temptation, accepts the skeptical conclusion, and presents an alternative theory that salvages what he thinks can be salvaged from the voice of temptation's intuitions.[18] But none of these voices is Wittgenstein himself.

On this analysis, Wittgenstein's role isn't to adjudicate between the voice of temptation and the voice of correctness, but to treat them both. Both are caught up in the idea that what the instructor has said isn't enough to convey her meaning—that it requires some kind of supplementation, interpretation—but, Wittgenstein observes,

> there is a way of grasping a rule which is *not* an interpretation, but which, from case to case of application, is exhibited in what we call 'following the rule' and 'going against it'. (*PI* §201)

Our charge, then, is to return to the everyday practice of rule-following, to examine the grey rags and dust without prejudice. When we do so, the situation with our recalcitrant pupil suddenly looks simple: if he writes 1004, we assume he's misunderstood; we give more examples, more explanations; if he doesn't get it right even then, we can't force him, but we do worry about his prospects; what we *don't* do is doubt that 1002 is correct. The facts are straightforward:

---

18. In other passages, the voice of temptation embraces mental states or infinitary mathematics and the voice of correctness responds with behaviorism or finitism.

> Following a rule is analogous to obeying an order. One is
> trained to do so, and one reacts to an order in a particular
> way. (*PI* §206)

If we didn't all react in much the same way, if lots of people
reacted as the imagined recalcitrant student does, our ways
of teaching and doing arithmetic would break down, but this
doesn't actually happen:

> Disputes do not break out . . . over the question of whether
> or not a rule has been followed. People don't come to blows
> over it. (*PI* §240)

As a matter of fact, we convey our meaning quite easily, and
the human practice of arithmetic carries on quite successfully.
And all this is open to view, uncontroversial, 'what everyone
would admit', just as Wittgenstein promised.

So the question for the Wittgensteinian therapist is what
keeps the voices of temptation and correctness from being
satisfied with these everyday observations. Once the question is posed this way, the answer emerges: when the skeptic
prompts them to imagine the recalcitrant student, when this
imaginary figure misunderstands one after another of the
instructor's explanations and examples, they forget about the
everyday world in which students do understand and begin to
think they need a way of teaching that simply can't be misunderstood, no matter how wayward the pupil; they're out to find
a way of specifying the rule, of conveying our meaning, that

will hit its mark no matter how outlandish the circumstances. As the influential Wittgenstein interpreter Cora Diamond puts it, they're after 'an account [that works when] addressed to someone on whose uptake, on whose responses, we are not at all depending' (Diamond [1986], pp. 68–69). The voice of temptation tries and fails at this; the voice of correctness gives up hope of a fact of the matter and settles for explaining how we get by with something less. What both miss are the ordinary facts that support perfectly workable notions of correctness and incorrectness for actual human beings in our world. 1000 plus 2 is 1002, and we all know it.[19]

My contention, then, is that something like this style of analysis ultimately carries over to Wittgenstein's treatment of skepticism in *On Certainty*, but first we need to consider a few facts about the composition and structure of that book. On the basis of extensive biographical, archival, and textual evidence, Brian Rogers [2011] has persuasively argued that the remarks compiled by the editors from Wittgenstein's final notebooks fall into three distinct periods: §§1–65, written either during or shortly after his visit to Ithaca in the fall of 1949; §§66–299, written during his treatment for the prostate cancer diagnosed when he returned to Cambridge; and §§300–676, written during his final two months, April and May of 1951, after treatment had been discontinued. This breakdown is philosophically significant because Wittgenstein was consistently dissatisfied

---

19. See [2014], pp. 63–73, 95–98, for more on this line of interpretation, with references.

with the work he produced during the latter part of 1949, as his then-undiagnosed illness worsened, and during the period of his treatment, despite the improvement in his overall physical well-being.[20] Only during those final two months did he feel that 'the curtain in my brain has gone up' and 'I suddenly found myself in the right frame of mind for doing philosophy'.[21] With this in mind, I propose to concentrate on the third part of *On Certainty*, the part Wittgenstein approved, but first a glance at his initial take on Moore in the opening sections, before his diagnosis and treatment.

The book begins with a reference to Moore's proof:

> If you do know that *here is one hand*, we'll grant you all the rest. When one says that such and such a proposition can't be proved, of course that does not mean that it can't be derived from other propositions; any proposition can be derived from other ones. But they may be no more certain than it is itself. (*OC* §1)

Presumably this is intended to cast doubt on the efficacy of the inference from 'here's a hand and here's another' to 'there are things outside us': the premise is no more certain than the conclusion. Soon Wittgenstein takes to schooling Moore on the nature of the skeptical challenge:

---

20. This is independently plausible, given that cloudy cognition is a known side effect of the kind of hormone treatment he was receiving.
21. From a letter to Malcolm dated April 16, 1951. See Wittgenstein [2011].

The statement 'I know that here is a hand' may then be continued: 'for it's *my* hand that I'm looking at'. Then a reasonable man will not doubt that I know.—Nor will the [skeptic]; rather he will say that he was not dealing with the practical doubt which is being dismissed, but there is a further doubt *behind* that one.—That this is an *illusion* has to be shewn in a different way. (*OC* §19)

The doubt behind the doubt must be the 'from scratch' challenge:

My believing the trustworthy man stems from my admitting that it is possible for him to make sure. But someone who says that perhaps there are no physical objects makes no such admission. (*OC* §23)

The skeptic 'is doubting the whole system of evidence' (*OC* §185).[22] Apparently unaware of Moore's 1933–1934 lectures, Wittgenstein imagines that Moore must take 'here's a hand' to be different in kind from scientific claims:

'Doubting the existence of the external world' does not mean for example doubting the existence of a planet, which later observations proved to exist.—Or does Moore want to say that knowing that here is his hand is different

22. Here I violate my self-imposed embargo of the middle section of *On Certainty*.

in kind from knowing the existence of the planet Saturn? Otherwise it would be possible to point out the discovery of the planet Saturn to the doubters and say that its existence has been proved, and hence the existence of the external world as well. (*OC*, §20)

Surely no one would think to infer the existence of bodies from the existence of, say, dinosaurs!

All this suggests that Wittgenstein takes Moore to have misunderstood the 'from scratch' challenge, so the first step in his treatment is to get Moore to see what his opponent wants and how what he, Moore, is offering is nowhere near satisfactory. I've been suggesting, on the contrary, that Moore understands quite well what's going on, that he's employing a strategy of putting the skeptic on the defensive by adopting the point of view of the Plain Man and the Plain Inquirer and in effect challenging the skeptic to explain what's wrong with it. But even if I'm right about this, the fact remains that Moore hasn't answered the 'from scratch' challenge—he's just trying to demonstrate that this failure doesn't threaten his ordinary beliefs. In any case, it's notable that Wittgenstein changes his take on Moore in the final portion of the book, during the writing of which he had a series of productive conversations with Moore himself in Cambridge. I think Wittgenstein still doesn't have Moore quite right, but leaving that aside, it's in these passages that the therapeutic reading I'm after finds its raw materials.

The picture of Moore in these late passages has him understanding the skeptical challenge and responding to it directly by saying 'I know that's a tree' in an extraordinary way (they've switched from 'here's a hand' to this example, apparently sitting in Moore's garden):[23]

> What I am aiming at is . . . found in the difference between the causal observation 'I know that that's a . . . ' as it might be used in ordinary life, and the same utterance when a philosopher makes it. (*OC* §406)
>
> For when Moore says 'I know that that's . . . ' I want to reply 'you don't know anything!'—and yet I would not say that to anyone who was speaking without philosophical intention. That is, I feel (rightly?) that these two mean to say something different. (*OC* §407)

Wittgenstein takes Moore to be 'speaking with philosophical intention', not simply with the Plain Man or the Plain Inquirer. And he thinks this usage is somehow problematic:

> When one hears Moore say 'I *know* that that's a tree', one suddenly understands those who think that that has by no means been settled. The matter strikes one all at once as being unclear and blurred. It is as if Moore had put it in the wrong light.

23. I have to share *OC*, §467: 'I am sitting with a philosopher in the garden; he says again and again "I know that that's a tree", pointing to a tree that is near us. Someone else arrives and hears this, and I tell him: "This fellow isn't insane. We are only doing philosophy"'.

It is as if I were to see a painting (say a painted stage-set) and recognize what it represents from a long way off at once and without the slightest doubt. But now I step nearer: and then I see a lot of patches of different colours, which are all highly ambiguous and do not provide any certainty whatever. (*OC* §481)

It is as if 'I know' did not tolerate a metaphysical emphasis. (*OC* §482)

The idea is that as the Plain Man or the Plain Inquirer use the sentence, it's perfectly in order, but when Moore tries to use it to refute the skeptic, it acquires 'metaphysical emphasis'—it is viewed too close up, it loses its force. Again, Moore as I understand him uses his sentences is a perfectly ordinary way, he isn't attempting a direct refutation of the 'from scratch' skeptic, but let's now shift our attention to Moore as Wittgenstein understands him in these final passages.

It's natural to see this Moore as embodying a voice of temptation: he thinks that's a tree; he's beset by the skeptic; he says, emphatically, that he *knows* it's a tree. So the voice of temptation is familiar, as it should be, but where is the voice of correctness? Just as in the case of rule-following, this theme is one that many interpreters take to be the view Wittgenstein himself is advocating.[24] It's introduced in the middle section, written

24. Unsurprisingly, these are often the very readers who deny that Wittgenstein is engaged in therapeutic philosophizing in *OC* (see footnote 14).

when Wittgenstein felt 'muddled and sluggish',[25] then turns up off and on throughout the final section, as would be expected if it were intended eventually for the voice of correctness.

The key idea for this voice is that Moore's various obvious claims should be regarded—not as he regards them (according to Wittgenstein), as ordinary claims issued with 'philosophical intent'—but as so-called 'hinge propositions':

> That is to say, the *questions* that we raise and our *doubts* depend on the fact that some propositions are exempt from doubt, are as it were like hinges on which those turn. (*OC* §341)

> 'Dispute about other things; *this* is immovable—it is a hinge on which your dispute can turn'. (*OC* §655)

For a fuller characterization, here are some illustrative passages from the middle section:

> I should like to say: Moore does not *know* what he asserts he knows, but it stands fast for him, as also fast for me; regarding it as absolutely solid is part of our *method* of doubt and enquiry. I do not explicitly learn the propositions that stand fast for me. I can *discover* them subsequently like the axis around which a body rotates. This axis is not fixed in the sense that anything holds it fast, but the movement around it determines its immobility. (*OC* §§151–152)

25. Letter of January 22, 1950, to Rhees. See Wittgenstein [2011].

The *truth* of certain empirical propositions belongs to our frame of reference. (*OC* §83)

It may be ... that *all enquiry on our part* is set so as to exempt certain propositions from doubt, if they are ever formulated. They lie apart from the route travelled by enquiry. (*OC* §88)

All testing, all confirmation and disconfirmation of a hypothesis takes place already within a system. And this system is not a more or less arbitrary and doubtful point of departure for all our arguments: no, it belongs to the essence of what we call an argument. The system is not so much the point of departure, as the element in which arguments have their life. (*OC* §105)

The thought is that claims like Moore's 'here is a hand' and 'that's a tree' look like ordinary empirical claims, but in fact they aren't confirmed—indeed, they can't be confirmed because they have to be in place in order for any confirmation or disconfirmation at all to be possible.

As in the rule-following case, this is a skeptical solution, because it accepts the skeptic's conclusion in his debate with the voice of temptation: Moore doesn't have evidence for his claim to have hands; the Plain Man can't confirm his belief in that chair. Nevertheless, the story goes, Moore and the Plain Man are perfectly within their rights to accept these claims, because they are part of the backdrop against which offering evidence and confirming take place. But of course Moore and the Plain Man *do* think they have good reason to believe what they believe: Moore feels and controls his hands; the Plain Man sees the chair right in front of him in broad daylight. If these ordinary bits of grey rags and dust are to be retained, we need to identify the shared presupposition that blocks both the voice of temptation and the voice of correctness from feeling their force.

Here I think the answer once again runs parallel to the rule-following case. There both the voice of temptation and the voice of correctness assume that a proper account of how the instructor meant the rule must be one that would pick out her intention no matter how bizarre the circumstances; it must work without depending on the ways humans actually react to training or the role of arithmetic in our lives. This time, both voices assume that proper evidence, the only truly acceptable evidence, must support the claim for which it's evidence no matter how bizarre the circumstances; it must work without depending on the contingent nature of our perceptual mechanisms, the actual makeup of the world we're perceiving, or anything else. Having implicitly accepted this starting point, the voice of temptation is boxed in by the skeptic, and the voice of correctness accepts the skeptic's contention that Moore and the Plain Man have no evidence, arguing that their claims lie outside the reach of evidence altogether—neither of which is an attractive resting place. What Wittgenstein suggests we do, is step back and revisit that implicit assumption: there's no good reason to demand that an explanation of meaning be independent of the human and worldly context for which it's intended; likewise, there's no good reason to demand a form of evidence that's independent of the human and worldly context in which it's being offered.[26] We don't need something that works no matter what; we just need something that works for us.

Wittgenstein's therapy is aimed at calling attention to, and thereby reducing the hold of, this kind of disconnect. He reminds us that knowing is something that happens in our actual interactions with our actual world:

> It is always by favour of Nature that one knows something.
> (OC §505)

In the case of knowledge, in the case of rule-following, and in other cases that Wittgenstein treats in other places,[27] the philosopher is repeatedly caught up in the same type of insidious presupposition:

> We have got on to slippery ice where there is no friction, and so, in a certain sense, the conditions are ideal; but also, just because of that, we are unable to walk. We want to walk: so we need *friction*. Back to the rough ground! (PI §107)

26. There may seem to be a disanalogy here, in that the grey rags and dust involve only human psychology in the rule-following case, but include features of the surrounding world in the case of skepticism. In fact, the cooperation of the world is also required in the case of meaning 'add-2': if objects routinely vanished or appeared (see *RFM*, §137), we couldn't have the stable arithmetical practices that we do.

27. Like logic. See [2014].

This is what happens when we find ourselves insisting on a type of evidence that would count toward the likelihood of our claim no matter how unusual the circumstances—and of course this is exactly what's going on when we ask for a kind of evidence that doesn't depend on any of our beliefs or methods, when we insist that no evidence is acceptable until extraordinary dreaming has been ruled out and the 'from scratch' challenge has been answered.

This seems to me an apt diagnosis of at least some of the forces that make the problem of radical skepticism so enduring. Wittgenstein's isolation of this more general quirk of philosophical psychology gives us a new perspective on the otherwise mysterious conviction that the lack of extraordinary evidence undercuts ordinary evidence: this general quirk, this desire for accounts that work 'no matter what', turns up in this case as the conviction that in fact only extraordinary evidence is legitimate. Whatever Wittgenstein's hopes may have been, I don't suppose these observations are likely to deter those actually gripped by the problem of radical skepticism, any more than Wittgenstein's own observations in the rule-following case have deterred those moved by his very own rule-following skepticism,[28] but they do help the rest of us understand the motivating forces behind it—and that, after all, was our goal.

Before we leave the topic of radical skepticism and think a bit about what, if anything, we've learned from all this

28. Miller and Wright [2002] or Kusch [2006] give a glimpse of how the debate has evolved.

about the practice of philosophy, I'd like to briefly revisit Wittgenstein's initial characterization of Moore in the early portion of *On Certainty*. This is the version of Moore who offers up his hands as proof of an external world without understanding the 'from scratch' nature of the skeptic's challenge. Of course I've suggested that in fact Moore understood just fine, that he was denying that his inability to meet the skeptic's terms casts doubt on his 'proof', and toward the end of *On Certainty*, Wittgenstein too takes Moore to understand and to be giving the claim about his hands some extra metaphysical oomph, but let's regress to that earlier understanding for a moment to explore a different puzzle: given where Wittgenstein ends up, the right response to the skeptic is to stick with the ordinary evidence—the grey rags and dust—and this is precisely what this innocent version of Moore does; why then is it so crucial to get the innocent Moore to understand the true nature of the skeptical challenge? On the face of it, one might think that the innocent Moore is quite healthy as he stands, that he's in need of no therapeutic intervention at all, so why should we strive to infect him with the illness? This would seem uncalled for, even if we do imagine we're in possession of the cure.

Curiously enough, one possible answer comes from another series of lectures, delivered by Wittgenstein in 1934–1935, just one year after Moore's intriguing lectures about dinosaurs. Our access to Wittgenstein's lectures comes not from his own papers, as in the case of Moore, but from a compilation by Alice

Ambrose of her contemporaneous notes with those of another attendee, Margaret Macdonald. Here's what Ambrose came up with:

> Philosophy may start from common sense but it cannot remain with common sense ... because the business of philosophy is to rid one of those puzzles which do not arise for common sense. No philosopher lacks common sense in ordinary life. So philosophers should not attempt to present [skeptical] positions, for example, as though they were absurd—by pointing out to a person who puts forward these positions that he does not really wonder whether the beef is real or whether it is an idea in his mind, whether his wife is real or whether only he is real. Of course he does not, and it is not a proper objection.

> You must not try to avoid a philosophical problem by appealing to common sense; instead, present it as it arises with most power. You must allow yourself to be dragged into the mire, and get out of it.

> Philosophy can be said to consist of three activities: to see the commonsense answer, to get yourself so deeply into the problem that the commonsense answer is unbearable, and to get from that situation back to the commonsense answer. But the commonsense answer in itself is no solution; everyone knows it. One must not in philosophy

attempt to short-circuit problems. (Wittgenstein [1934/35], pp. 108–109)[29]

This may sound odd, Wittgenstein demeaning the answers that 'everyone knows', but perhaps his intent in the *Investigations* passage—'If someone were to advance *theses* in philosophy, it would never be possible to debate them, because everyone would agree to them' (*PI* §128)—is just to emphasize that stating theses is not what philosophy properly does. What philosophy properly does is cure illnesses, and it does this by returning us to common sense, but the crucial point is: no illness, no philosophy.

This strikes me as a sadly crimped view of the philosophical project, as it would Reid, Moore, or Austin. What the innocent Moore and the Plain Man say to the skeptic is entirely in order, and my not-so-innocent Moore and the Plain Inquirer are prepared to issue a challenge of their own: explain why my lack of extraordinary evidence undercuts my ordinary evidence. Likewise,

---

29. See also Wittgenstein [1933/34], pp. 58–59: 'One can defend common sense against the attacks of philosophers only by solving their problems, i.e., by curing them of the temptation to attack common sense; not by restating the views of common sense. A philosopher is not a man out of his senses, a man who doesn't see what everybody sees; nor on the other hand is his disagreement with common sense that of the scientist disagreeing with the coarse view of the man in the street. That is, his disagreement is not founded on a more subtle knowledge of fact. We therefore have to look round for the *source* of his puzzlement'. This comes from *The Blue Book*, a set of notes Wittgenstein dictated during 1933–1934, the very years of Moore's lectures. The subtitle refers to this as a 'preliminary study for the *Philosophical Investigations*'. (Thanks to Brian Rogers and Curtis Sommerlatte for calling this passage and the one in the text to my attention.)

what Austin, Reid, and the Plain Inquirer say in response to the Argument from Illusion is also to the point: common sense and vision science can deal with all the usual cases without any call for sense data. If more is wanted, if we hope to understand why the skeptic regards these answers as unsatisfactory, then various diagnostic enterprises are certainly in order, from Austin's taxonomy of mostly verbal distortions, to the anachronistic influence of early modern vision science, to Reid's isolation of semi-skepticism and its weaknesses, to Wittgenstein's excavation of his own strange quirk of philosophical psychology. But this is hardly the only job for the philosopher—which brings us back at last to the question from which we started: what do philosophers do?

3. BEYOND

We started our investigation of philosophy and its methods with a sample of a typically philosophical question: how do we come to know anything at all about the world around us? This led us into the debate over radical skepticism and ultimately to the conclusion that the enduring appeal of the skeptical arguments is largely a consequence of various argumentative slips, verbal distortions, anachronistic theorizing, unmotivated presuppositions, and plain acts of inattention and carelessness. If this sort of thing is all philosophy has to offer, then maybe Wittgenstein was right, maybe our central job should be just to look for cures!

It will come as no surprise that I don't think this is the right moral to draw. To illustrate, let's glance back at the other two samples of typically philosophical questions that were floated at the beginning. One was: what makes 2 + 2 equal to 4? More generally, we might ask: what is mathematics about?, is it like a natural science, describing a particular sort of thing, like botany or astronomy, or is it some other kind of activity altogether?, mathematicians justify their claims by proving them, but what justifies the assumptions from which those proofs begin? These aren't properly mathematical questions, though the answers may bear on mathematical activity; they don't seem to be questions that can be answered by finding out more empirical facts about the world, though mathematics is obviously an indispensable tool for scientific progress. These questions don't fall within some established discipline, or I should say, they don't fall within any established discipline other than philosophy!

The other sample from the beginning was this: why is it that a coin that comes up either heads or tails, but doesn't come up heads, must come up tails? Drawing this sort of conclusion is normally called 'logical inference'—it strikes us as the most reliable sort of inference there is, but why? What does its apparently exceptional reliability rest on? Is it something about the world, about us, about our language? These, too, are questions that we need to answer if we're to fully understand the world, ourselves included. But, again, they're questions no other discipline is out to claim. They fall to philosophy.

Now there are, no doubt, ways of approaching these questions that are hopelessly intertwined with the kinds of distortions and confusions and fallacies that we've seen in such great

profusion surrounding the question of radical skepticism—
ways of approaching them that do stand in need of diagnosis,
treatment, and cure. For example, before the inquiry even
begins, the requirement of necessity is often imposed: mathematical and logical claims have to turn out to be correct not
only in this world but in any possible world. Given what we've
been through in these lectures, I suspect this thought starts the
little hairs to rising on the back of your neck—only grief can
come of insisting on this sort of thing from the start, before one
even begins to look around. But the fact that there are bad ways
to go about addressing questions like these doesn't imply that
all ways of addressing them are bad, and it's the philosopher's
job to find the good ones.

When we look at the matter this way, we see that in fact the
question we've been stalking all this time—how do we come
to know anything at all about the world?—is itself a perfectly
good question; what led us to grief was approaching it in various
ways that ended us up in skepticism. Looking back at Berkeley
and Reid, we recall their serious and productive investigations of the mechanisms underlying our sensory information
about the world, especially visual information, investigations
that helped determine the eventual shape of contemporary
vision theory. In fact, the rise of early modern philosophy was
largely a reaction to the scientific revolution, to the new science of the time—really the beginning of science as we now
understand the term. This transformation is generally dated to
Copernicus, who published his heliocentric model in 1543; it
was marked by the rise of rigorous empirical and experimental

methods—Galileo, Bacon—and the development and application of advanced mathematics, culminating in Newton's *Principia* (1687); its effects profoundly reoriented everything from astronomy, physics, chemistry, and optics, to the study of electricity and the theory and practice of medicine.

Descartes, as we've seen, was out to provide a philosophical foundation for the new mechanistic science, to replace the old Aristotlian Scholasticism. Locke actually worked in the laboratory of Robert Boyle, the man credited with founding modern chemistry as it emerged from alchemy. (You may remember Boyle's law, about the inverse relation of pressure and volume in a gas.) Locke describes his role this way:

> The Commonwealth of Learning, is not at this time without Master-Builders, whose mighty Designs, in advancing the Sciences, will leave lasting Monuments to the Admiration of Posterity; But every one must not hope to be a Boyle . . . and in an Age that produces such Masters as . . . the incomparable Mr. Newton . . . 'tis Ambition enough to be employed as an Under-Labourer in clearing Ground a little, and removing some of the Rubbish, that lies in the way to Knowledge. (Locke [1689], Epistle to the Reader, pp. 9–10)

What Locke is out to clear away is the outmoded but still lingering notions, jargon, and conceptual confusions of Scholasticism. But he's also out to explore and assess the relevance of the Boyle's corpuscular science for the understanding of our perceptual and cognitive relations to the world.[30] Reid, as we've seen, draws heavily on the science of his time and even engaged in experimentation of his own. All these philosophers approached our question—how do we come to know anything at all about the world?—very much in the scientific spirit of the time, trying to understand how human beings manage to register reliable information about the world.

It might well surprise these thinkers to see how contemporary philosophers approach that same question: for many epistemologists of our day, the emphasis isn't on how we manage to form reliable beliefs but on the concept of 'knowledge'. The central question has become—'under what conditions is it correct to say that someone knows?' and discussion is dominated by commentary on ever-more-complex problem cases,[31] beginning with the Gettier example noted in the first lecture: you believe I own a Chevy because you see me driving

30. For example, his famous distinction between primary and secondary qualities (e.g., shape vs. color) is so closely intertwined with Boylean corpuscularism that in his presentation, Locke apologizes ([1689], II.8.22, p. 140): 'I have . . . been engaged in Physical Enquiries a little farther than, perhaps, I intended. But it [is] necessary, to make the Nature of Sensation a little understood'.

31. Here's a recent example, from Sosa [2009], p. 186: 'Suppose I fancy myself a connoisseur of tomato ripeness, but suffer from a rare form of color blindness that precludes my discerning nearly any shade of red except that displayed by this particular tomato. Therefore my judgments of tomato ripeness are in general apt to be right with no better than even chance. But when it's the particular (and rare) shade of red now displayed, then I am nearly infallible. Oblivious to my affliction, however, I issue judgments of tomato ripeness with abandon over a wide spectrum of shades of red. Assuming that, unknown to me, the variety of tomato involved always ripens with this shape of red, then my belief that this tomato is ripe is in step with the truth'. So, do I or do I not know that this tomato is ripe? Would it make a difference if only this variety of tomato is found in my general neighborhood? (Recall footnote 48 of Lecture I.)

one to work every day; I do own a Chevy, but the one you've seen me drive to work belongs to my sister; can you properly be said to know I own a Chevy? Descartes, Locke, Berkeley, and Reid would no doubt be baffled by our contemporary fixation on questions like this one. Nowadays, even those who advocate a role for science in epistemology often take the philosopher's job to be the initial one of analyzing the concept of 'knowledge' to determine what it is—after which that analysis is handed off to the scientist to settle how and where instances of 'knowledge' are to be found in the world. In contrast, our early moderns would presumably be disinclined to relinquish their own role in empirical inquiry, from the helpful ground-clearing of Locke to the active involvement of Descartes, Berkeley, and Reid. They would all mostly likely think that the fundamental task of epistemology has gotten lost in odd diversionary issues.

Now I suspect many would say that this stark contrast between contemporary and early modern approaches can be explained by the very success of scientific activity from Copernicus to the present day. Just as chemistry emerged from alchemy in the 17th century, empirical psychology emerged from philosophy in the 19th century, and contemporary descendants of Descartes, Locke, Berkeley, and Reid now ply their trade in departments of cognitive science and the like. So it's only to be expected that professional philosophers would move on to new conceptual frontiers. Austin gave poetic voice to this sentiment in 1956:

In the history of human inquiry, philosophy has taken the place of the initial central sun, seminal and tumultuous:

from time to time, it throws off some portion of itself to take station as a science, a planet, cool and well regulated, progressing steadily towards a distant final state. This happened long ago at the birth of mathematics, and again at the birth of physics: only in the last century we have witnessed the same process once again, slow and at the time almost imperceptible, in the birth of the science of mathematical logic, through the joint labours of philosophers and mathematicians. Is it not possible that the next century may see the birth, through the joint labours of philosophers, grammarians and numerous other students of language, of a true and comprehensive *science of language*? Then we shall have rid ourselves of one more part of philosophy (there will still be plenty left) in the only way we ever can get rid of philosophy, by kicking it upstairs. (Austin [1956a], p. 232)

Austin was imagining the emergence of the science of linguistics, and indeed Noam Chomsky's revolutionary *Syntactic Structures* was published the very next year, in 1957. A similar story could be told about contemporary vision science, which arose out of psychology, computer science, and neuroscience, along with earlier philosophical theories, in the 1970s.

This picture has considerable appeal, along with a kernel of truth, but I think we have to concede that even Austin didn't quite believe what he was saying; after all, we know that he recognized at least one other way of 'getting rid of philosophy', namely by 'dissolving' philosophical problems, as he did in *Sense and Sensabilia*. But more to the present point, are those planetary spin-offs really so 'cool and well-regulated', are they really entirely beyond the need of any 'under-laboring'? In fact there remain difficult foundational questions in mathematics (for example, the one noted above about how to defend its fundamental assumptions), in physics (for example, the well-known conundra of quantum mechanics), in logic (for example, the question of what makes logical truths true), and of course in psychology (for example, what is the physical basis of phenomenal experience?)—all questions on which philosophers are still called upon to help out.[32] For that matter, there are important recent examples of the work of philosophers migrating directly into the sciences, much as Berkeley's and Reid's did in times gone by: Wittgenstein's notion of a 'family resemblance concept' is now a cornerstone of the empirical study of human conceptualization; Austin's analysis of 'speech acts' made its way into linguistics and computer science;[33]

32. The first case, from mathematics, has been my own bailiwick (see, e.g., [2011]). In the foundations of physics, see, e.g., the interaction of philosophers and physicists in Saunders et al. [2010]. The interdisciplinary character of contemporary logic is demonstrated by the membership of the international Association for Symbolic Logic, the leading professional organization in the field, which consists largely of mathematical logicians, computer scientists, and philosophers. See Hatfield and Allred [2012] for a recent interdisciplinary collection on vision science. Finally the preface to Metzinger [2000] begins: 'This volume ... unites a number of highly renowned neuroscientists and philosophers, from all over the world, who are together investigating the way in which the content of subjective experience is correlated with events in the brain' (p. vii).

33. See Austin [1955]. Here again, as so often, Reid is an important precursor. See Schuhmann and Smith [1990].

the work of various contemporary analytic philosophers has shaped thinking about the 'object concept' in developmental psychology.

So I think there can be little doubt that 'good' philosophical questions remain and that contemporary philosophy engages with science just as closely and productively as did the philosophy of the 17th and 18th centuries. The final question, then, is how these 'good' questions are best addressed, what methods are appropriate and effective. We've touched on an array of different approaches along the way; now it's time to take stock.

Let's start with the Plain Man, the fellow who claims to know there's a chair before him when it sees it there in broad daylight. The Plain Man may be confused by the skeptical argumentation, but he remains unruffled, confident something must have gone wrong somewhere. Reid's philosopher of common sense puts it this way:

> A traveler of good judgment may mistake his way, and be unawares led into a wrong track; and while the road is fair before him, he may go on without suspicion . . . but when it ends in a coal-pit, it requires no great judgment to know that he hath gone wrong. (Reid [1764], I.8, p. 23)

Reid continues, '. . . to know he hath gone wrong, *nor perhaps to find out what misled him*' (emphasis added). This further task belongs not to the Plain Man, who's perfectly within his rights to retain his belief in his chair, but to the Plain Inquirer. She's curious about all aspects of the world, including her perceptual access to it, so she needs to examine and assess the case for skepticism just as we've been doing here.

In terms of method, the Plain Inquirer conducts an ordinary empirical investigation: beginning from everyday observation, progressing to systematic gathering of data and deliberate experimentation, then eventually to theory formation and testing, always circling back to reassess and improve her methods as she learns more about the world and her interactions with it. What's striking is that all the 'good' philosophical questions we've identified here will come to her attention sooner or later: they're all things she'll want to know about in her tireless pursuit of a full understanding of human beings and their surroundings.[34] Furthermore, from what we've seen of her doings, including those of Reid and others in this spirit, she has the resources to find the answers: no unusual, exclusively philosophical methods appear to be required. As a first pass, I think it's reasonable to conclude that the Plain Inquirer's methods are proper and appropriate, even admirably effective.

Another approach we considered is Austin's ordinary language philosophizing:[35] explore 'what we would say when' to

---

34. E.g., the Plain Inquirer (in the person of the Second Philosopher) confronts that status of logical truth in [2007], Part III, [2014], and [2014a], and the defense of mathematical axioms in [2011].

35. Here we find yet another point of contact between Austin and Reid: 'The language of mankind is expressive of their thoughts, and of various operations of their minds. The various operations of the understanding, will, and passions,

uncover the subtleties and distinctions and hard-won wisdom embedded in our use of ordinary terms.[36] We've seen that Austin recommends this approach only in cases 'where ordinary language is rich and subtle, as it is in the pressingly practical matter of excuses' (Austin [1956], p. 182), but not 'when our interests are more extensive or intellectual than the ordinary', where we might have recourse to 'the microscope and its successors' (ibid., p. 185). The topic of excuses in particular draws Austin's attention because it is 'neighboring, analogous or germane in some way to some notorious centre of philosophical

which are common to mankind, have various forms of speech corresponding to them in all languages, which are signs of them, and by which they are expressed: And a due attention to the signs may, in many cases, give considerable light to the things signified by them' (Reid [1785], I.5, p. 56). (For a bit more, see [2011b], pp. 16–18.) Appeals to the facts of natural language recur throughout Reid [1764] and [1785], though his focus is on general characteristics of human cognition and for that reason most often on features shared by many different human languages.

36. So-called 'experimental philosophy' is a contemporary school that also explores what we would say when' (see, e.g., Alexander [2012]), but with very different goals and methods. Where Austin is out to explore the subtle ins and outs of word usage, the experimental philosopher takes himself to be charting the contours of a concept. Austin gathers like-minded colleagues on his 'Saturday mornings' (see Warnock [1973]) to consider a single term: by comparing it with various nearby terms (using a dictionary, including etymologies); by concocting, discussing, elaborating, and revising many scenarios; by working toward a group consensus. The experimental philosopher concocts a small number of scenarios and conducts a proper survey of how a large group of subjects would classify them. So, e.g., on intentional action, the experimental philosopher's survey would ask the subject whether the described action is 'intentional' or 'unintentional', while Austin's group might well end up concluding that neither term is quite right, that 'heedless' or 'negligent' or 'careless' would be better, and that demanding a choice the original two options is to embrace an 'overly tidy dichotomy'. I suspect that a serious comparison of the strengths and weaknesses of the two approaches would be quite fruitful.

trouble'—he has in mind Freedom, Responsibility, and Blame—but at the same time

> not too much trodden into bogs or tracks by traditional philosophy, for in that case even 'ordinary' language will often have become infected with the jargon of extinct theories, and our own prejudices too, as the upholders or imbibers of theoretical views, will be too readily, and often insensibly, engaged. . . . we can discuss at least clumsiness, or absence of mind, or inconsiderateness, even spontaneousness, without remembering what Kant thought, and so progress by degrees even to discussing deliberation without for once remembering Aristotle or self-control without Plato. (Austin [1956], pp. 182–183)

In this way, 'the philosophical study . . . can get off to a positive fresh start' (ibid., p. 180). Austin applies this same technique in 'Ifs and cans' (Austin [1956a])—as in 'I *can* do this, *if* I so choose'—with Free Will as the nearby 'centre of philosophical trouble'. J. O. Urmson, one of the editors of Austin's papers, reports that

> Austin regarded [his ordinary language] method as empirical and scientific, one that could lead to definitely established results, but he admitted that 'like most sciences, it is an art', and that a suitably fertile imagination was all important for success. (Urmson [1969], p. 25)

All this falls well within the reach of the Plain Inquirer.

Though Austin made positive application of ordinary language philosophizing in investigations like these and in speech act theory, the applications we've seen in these lectures have mostly been therapeutic. This is explicit in *Sense and Sensabilia*, where the goal is to heal the poor philosopher in the grip of the Argument from Illusion, but the discussion of 'know' in 'Other minds' can also be seen as therapeutic in retrospect: the hope is that the skeptic will come to appreciate the many virtues of our everyday use of 'know' and elect to stick with it.

I think everything we've seen here indicates that therapeutic methods in general can be genuinely beneficial. We're all better off guarding against overly tidy dichotomies, dangerously narrow selections of carelessly described examples, undefined technical terms, especially when they're masquerading as familiar words, and so on. When we find ourselves with inconsistent convictions, when we feel compelled while philosophizing to reject what seems perfectly reasonable in ordinary life, we do well to ask whether we're making some unnoticed prejudicial assumption that's sapping the force of our familiar and effective ways of doing things. And I think our explorations have also revealed the importance of examining the historical roots of a given philosophical persuasion, to see whether it might have been generated by constraints that are no longer with us: for example, Locke's notion that everything in human cognition must enter through immediate sensory experience was a reasonable psychological hypothesis at the time, but we now know much more about how the structures of the brain and the sensory systems have evolved to exploit worldly regularities, in a sense relying on information that doesn't come to us in Locke's way. Once again, all these insights are accessible to ordinary empirical investigation; therapeutic philosophizing is another perfectly suitable instrument for the Plain Inquirer's toolkit.

Of the methods we've touched on, then, the odd man out, alas, is the cornerstone of contemporary analytic philosophy: conceptual analysis. We've had a few glimpses of how this plays out in the case of knowledge, the most conspicuous application these days, and the view hasn't been particularly edifying. The Plain Inquirer is sympathetic to Austin's idea that there is no 'concept of knowledge', only an intricate array of subtle and effective uses of the word 'know'—and there's no reason to suppose that these facts of actual usage are determinate enough to settle the ever-more-complex puzzles of Gettierology (sometimes, as we've seen, 'words fail us'[37]). Viewing the debate through the early modern eyes of Descartes, Locke, Berkeley, and Reid, we see it as drawing attention away from the central question of how we manage to acquire reliable information about the world.

Realities like these have led some philosophers sympathetic to science-oriented approaches like the Plain Inquirer's to reject the whole program of conceptual analysis as misconceived from the start. This seems to me too quick, because there are important cases in the history of science that might naturally be described

---

37. See footnote 48 of Lecture I.

as 'conceptual analysis'. One example from mathematics is Richard Dedekind's study of the notion of 'continuity', which lay at the basis of the infinitesimal calculus (Dedekind [1872]). When Dedekind was writing, in the late 19th century, the calculus had been around for two hundred years since Newton invented it—in the process of revolutionizing physics with the laws of motion and universal gravitation—but its fundamental notions still weren't clearly understood, and its theorems weren't rigorously proved. Dedekind hoped this could be remedied by pining down precisely what it is to say that a line is continuous, and he came up with this: if you divide the points on the line into two groups so that every point in one group is to the left of every point in the other, then there must be a single point that's either rightmost on the left-hand group or leftmost on the right-hand group; in intuitive terms, if you slice the line in two there has to be a point there. This is a precise way of expressing the intuitive idea that the line is continuous because it has no gaps. (Before Dedekind, mathematicians had relied on vague ideas like this: if you draw it, you don't have to lift your pencil off the page.) Dedekind's account not only provided a key ingredient in the rigorous foundation for the calculus, it also led to fruitful generalizations in what's now known as topology. No right-minded Plain Inquirer would want to do without this![38]

Another example comes from Einstein's analysis of the notion of simultaneity in the special theory of relativity.[39] The

---

38. The Plain Inquirer's (positive) attitude toward mathematics is examined in [2011].
39. Here I follow Einstein's popular presentation in his [1961].

problem he faced was an apparent contradiction between two well-confirmed facts: the principle of relativity—if one frame of reference is moving uniformly with respect to another, then the physical laws are the same in both—and the principle that the speed of light is constant.[40] Much as Dedekind asked what it is to be 'continuous', Einstein asked what it is to be 'simultaneous', and he came up with this: two momentary events are simultaneous if, when I stand midway between them, I see both at once. On this analysis, it turns out that if one frame of reference is moving uniformly with respect to another, two events that are simultaneous in the first needn't be simultaneous in the other.[41] With this 'relativity of simultaneity', the apparent conflict is no longer derivable.[42] Again, this is surely something the Plain Inquirer will approve and applaud.

What distinguishes, then, between the cases where conceptual analysis is clearly productive and the cases where it seems a dubious distraction? I think the answer is threefold: the targets of analysis, the methods of analysis, and the criteria of success for an analysis, all have a different character. In the

---

40. Imagine a train moving at constant velocity v along the tracks. If you stand beside the tracks and shine a flashlight in the same direction as the train is moving, the velocity of light from your frame of reference is c, but from the train's frame of reference, it's $c-v$.

41. Suppose two flashes of light A and B are simultaneous for you (in the sense in the text) as you stand beside the tracks. Inside the train as it travels from the location of A toward the location of B, the light from flash B will arrive ahead of the light from flash A, so they aren't simultaneous.

42. Because the argument in footnote 40 that the speed of your flashlight beam, viewed from inside the train, is $c-v$ depends on the assumption that times in the two frames of reference can be freely interchanged.

mathematical and scientific cases, the candidate for analysis is a vague but workable notion that already plays an important theoretical role, a rough and ready intuitive picture that's been doing a good job in the theory so far, but isn't up to the new and more exacting demands now being placed upon it. The analyst's goal, then, is to make the notion more precise, or more accurately, to replace the notion with something more precise. In contrast, in the philosophical cases, the candidate for analysis is 'that object or idea . . . that the word is generally used to stand for', as Moore puts it (Moore [1903], §6), what Stroud calls 'the ordinary concept', and the analyst's job is to learn, to discover, more about the preexisting objective contours of the concept.

The methods used to carry out the analysis also differ. Moore's method is to propose a set of conditions that may capture the concept; to examine and concoct an array of test cases in search of examples that we all agree satisfy the conditions but don't fall under the concept, or vice versa; to amend the conditions in light of these examples; and to repeat this process until no false positives or false negatives can be found. Dedekind and Einstein engage in no such process; they simply call on their great mathematical or physical understanding to formulate a new, more precise notion. And finally, the criteria for success. In the mathematical and scientific cases, these are clear and exacting: if Dedekind's analysis hadn't made it possible to prove the theorems that found the calculus, if Einstein's analysis hadn't removed the apparent contradiction between the principle of relativity and the constant speed of light, then they would have failed. What counts as success in the philosophical case is more elusive: the goal is to track, not word usage, but the facts about something that purportedly corresponds to that usage, something whose very existence Austin has led us to doubt.

Given these contrasts, it appears that Austin was right to distinguish cases like 'excuses' from cases like 'time', and to think that 'know' belongs with 'excuses', not with 'time'. Both 'know' and 'excuses' are fields 'where ordinary language is rich and subtle . . . pressingly practical' (Austin [1956], p. 182); both 'continuity' and 'simultaneity' (or 'time') are fields where 'our interests are more extensive or intellectual than the ordinary' (ibid., p. 185).

The epistemologist, Hilary Kornblith would disagree, placing 'know' instead with 'continuity' and 'time':

> When we seek to explain the presence of various cognitive capacities in a species . . . knowledge enters the picture. . . . The environment makes certain informational demands on a species, and cognitive capacities answer to those demands. They are reliable capacities for the uptake of information about the environment. . . . Animals ignorant of their surroundings are less likely to . . . survive. There is thus a good deal of evolutionary pressure on a species in favor of reliable cognitive capacities for the production of true belief. (Kornblith [2007], p. 47).

The argument from 'instilled by evolution' to 'largely truth-tracking' has been a popular one among philosophers[43]—the

43. See, e.g., Quine [1969], p. 126: 'creatures inveterately wrong in their inductions have a pathetic but praiseworthy tendency to die before reproducing their kind'.

contemporary counterpart to Descartes's conviction that a benevolent deity wouldn't give us deceptive faculties—but it's now widely recognized that what's adaptive may not in fact track the truth: it may be more conducive to survival for our faculties to make quick and inaccurate judgments—just as a benevolent deity might engage in paternalistic deception,[44] or our parents might tell us untruths on occasion, for our own good. But leaving this aside, the real-world phenomenon that Kornblith points to is reliable cognition, and we could have all the information possible about how that works without settling the Gettierological subtleties of which instances of such cognition count as 'knowledge'. So the worldly item Kornblith is out to study—reliable cognition—doesn't appear to be what the epistemologist wants analyzed—the concept of knowledge.

All this suggests, or at least I'm inclined to draw, several conclusions: that there is a difference in kind between everyday terms like 'know' and 'excuse', and theoretical terms like 'continuity' and 'simultancity'; that conceptual analysis of the usual philosophical sort is a quite different undertaking from the conceptual analyses in our theoretical examples; that ordinary language investigation, not conceptual analysis, is appropriate in the everyday cases; that conceptual analysis of the theoretical sort, not philosophical analysis or ordinary language investigation, is appropriate for the theoretical terms.

44. Reid claims only that the Almighty provides us the faculties we need 'in order to our supplying the wants of nature, and avoiding the dangers to which we are constantly exposed' (Reid [1785], II.5, p. 101), allowing (unlike Descartes) for the possibility of paternalistic deception. See de Bary [2002], chapter 10, for this interpretation of Reid.

There's no ground here for rejecting conceptual analysis altogether, but its effective application appears to be somewhat different, and more circumscribed, than the doctrine of 'philosophy as analysis' might lead one to believe.

So, finally, what have we learned about philosophy? I hope we've learned that there are genuine philosophical questions of more than one variety: questions without a home in any other discipline, like 'if a coin comes up heads or tails, but it doesn't come up heads, why must it come up tails?'; questions destined to spin off into other disciplines, like 'what is the world made of?' or 'what is time?'; questions that arise inside other disciplines, like 'what worldly reality accounts for the success of quantum mechanics?' or 'how can a fundamental assumption of mathematics be defended?' I hope we've also learned that a philosopher can operate quite successfully from the point of view of the Plain Man and the Plain Inquirer, employing just common sense and ordinary empirical methods. These empirical methods can, with advantage, include some more specialized tools, like ordinary language investigations, appropriate conceptual analyses, and therapeutic cautions against pitfalls like a too quick or unnoticed slide from the everyday to the 'in principle'. As long as there are humans, an inherently curious species, there will be those who want to understand everything they can about the world and our place it in—there will be Plain Inquirers, trying to answer questions like these. And *this*, I submit, is what philosophers do best.

APPENDIX A

The Infinite Regress of Justification

The oldest argument for radical skepticism comes to us from Sextus Empiricus, writing in the second century AD, most likely drawing on the teachings of the otherwise-unknown Agrippa from around the year 0. The idea is simple and familiar:

> What is brought forward as a source of conviction for the matter proposed itself needs another such source, which itself needs another, and so *ad infinitum*, so that we have no point from which to begin to establish anything, and suspension of judgement follows. (Sextus [200], I.166)

Only two apparent alternatives to this infinite regress present themselves:

> The Dogmatists . . . begin from something which they do not establish but claim to assume simply and without proof. (Ibid., I.168)

> The reciprocal mode occurs when what ought to be confirmatory of the object under investigation needs to be made convincing by the object under

investigation; then, being unable to take either in order to establish the other, we suspend judgment about both. (Ibid., I.169)

Here we have Agrippa's famous trilemma: the attempt to justify any claim ends in something unjustified, runs in a circle, or generates an infinite regress.

In contemporary epistemology, these three horns are customarily associated with three general schools of thought on the structure of justification. Foundationalism opts for what Sextus calls Dogmatism: some claims don't require justification in terms of others (either because they somehow justify themselves or because they're justified some other way that doesn't appeal to other claims). Often those 'basic' claims are taken to be 'inner'—claims about sense data, for example—which generates the type of skepticism explored in Lecture II, the demand for an inference from inner to outer. Coherentism rejects the underlying idea that justification is a linear (or even branching) process in favor of a holistic 'web' of mutual support.[1] There the skeptical worry is that there could be many quite different internally coherent systems, that coherence alone can't be counted on to capture the way the world actually is. Finally, Infinitism attempts to exonerate the infinite regress—my belief in p is based on my belief in p_1, which is based on my belief in p_2, which is based on my belief in p_3, and so on—which is no doubt a tough assignment: at each point in the process, we're relying on claims with no basis, so 'we have no point from which to begin to establish anything' (Sextus [200], §166).[2]

Much subtle and ingenious philosophizing has grown up around Agrippa's problem. What matters for our purposes is that the Plain Inquirer

1. Coherentism is often thought of as the contemporary position that corresponds to the circular mode, but it's really best viewed as rejecting a structured picture of justification altogether, in favor of the web of belief.
2. As far as I know, it wasn't until the late 1990s that it occurred to anyone to try to defend this position—many hundreds of years after Sextus, not to mention Agrippa! See Klein [1999] or Turri and Klein [2014].

does see herself as duty bound to provide evidence for any of her beliefs, so the question of how those evidential relations are structured is a real one for her. So let's recall what she says when challenged on her belief in the Plain Man's chair—viewed at close range in broad daylight—and see what structure can be discerned there.[3]

We've noted (in I.2) that she begins her defense just as the Plain Man does, saying that she sees the chair there. She then calls attention to the various surrounding conditions that make for reliable vision: the lighting is good, the chair is only a few feet away, it isn't occluded or oddly situated; her eyes are open, she's well-rested, she's not under the influence of hallucinogens; and so on. Any one of these beliefs can be challenged. 'Why do you think that your belief is an ordinary visual belief?' She replies: Because the accompanying experience is interrupted when I close my eyes; because the belief has a characteristic richness, not just reporting the chair before me, but also its shape, color, orientation, and more; because it shifts in predictable ways as I move; and so on. 'How do you know all this about your experience?' Because I've checked for the various ways in which introspection goes wrong: for example, I'm attending carefully; I'm not hurried or distressed; the chair is right in front of me, so I'm not calling on peripheral vision where we often make mistakes about what we think we see, etcetera. 'Why do you think central vision is more reliable than peripheral vision?' Because the fovea (central area) of the retina has more receptors ... and so on.

3. Austin argues that claims don't bear evidential relations to one another in isolation, that what supports what depends on the context: e.g., 'it is not true in general that statements of how things are are "based on" statements of how things appear, look, or seem and not vice versa. I may say, for instance, "That pillar is bulgy" on the ground that it looks bulgy; but equally I might say, in different circumstances, "That pillar looks bulgy"—on the ground that I've just built it, and I *built* it bulgy' (Austin [1962], pp. 116–117). I take for granted that the context of the challenge to the Plain Man's belief about the chair and the kind of evidence the Plain Inquirer takes to be relevant are sufficiently well specified.

In all this, she never reaches anything like the Foundationalist's basic beliefs: even the simplest perceptual or introspective belief can be further defended, along the lines indicated. But her justificatory pathways are also much more structured than the Coherentist's web: some of her beliefs do provide evidence for others; justification doesn't just arise all at once from the way her many beliefs cohere. In fact, given the complexity of the ever-widening array of evidence she goes on to provide, both the linear or simply branching model and the picture of holistic web seem inadequate descriptive tools. Portrayed schematically, the Plain Inquirer's defense begins with the claim that she has a particular perceptual belief. Two further challenges arise: 'Why do you think you're having a perceptual belief of this kind?'—challenging her factual claim—and 'So what?'—challenging the relevance of the fact, even if granted. She responds to the first challenge by ruling out the conditions known to contribute to introspective error; she responds to the second by ruling out the conditions for perceptual error. Here she's already entered into some fairly detailed theorizing, and it won't be long before she's repeating the whole of vision science. What is the structure of this process? Does it come to an end somewhere?

One conspicuous feature of the Plain Inquirer's defense of her perceptual belief is that it rests in turn on quite a number of other perceptual claims, namely, those appealed to along the way in testing the many individual hypotheses of vision science. There's no direct circularity here, given that the perceptual claim about the chair presumably isn't itself included in the evidence offered for the science, but suppose we chose instead to challenge one of the perceptual claims that *is* present among the confirmations offered for the science—say a particular meter reading at a particular time—and ask the Plain Inquirer to defend *that* one? If she eventually repeats that big block of evidence, the whole of vision science, then one small part of the defense of the meter-reading claim will be that very meter-reading claim itself! Of course no single experiment is essential, any experiment should be replicable, so she could simply replace that particular meter-reading claim with another. Still, it can't be denied that at some level of description, perception is being used to assess the reliability of perception. If there's an Agrippan mode in play here, it's apparently the circular argument.

The fact that defending the reliability of perception seems to require appeal to perception has hardly been overlooked by epistemologists. Responses often take the form of a so-called 'track record' argument. The premises of such an argument include a list of things I believe—'there's a chair in front of me', 'there's a tree in the garden', 'here's a hand'—and the observation that I've formed a perceptual belief about each of them, in other words, a series of claims of the form: I have a perceptual belief that p, and p. From a long list of premises like this, it follows that perception has a good 'track record', that it's reliable! Though the conclusion— perception is reliable—isn't included directly among the premises, there is a sort of circularity here: to defend my premises, I'd have to appeal to my conclusion. Advocates of this approach[4] have developed a dramatic reply: in order for me to know my premises, perception has to *be* reliable, but I can know those premises without *knowing* that perception is reliable. This is called 'externalism', because whether or not I know depends on facts that may be unknown to me—in this case, the plain fact that perception is reliable. So if perception is in fact reliable, I can come to know the premises, correctly draw the conclusion, and thereby come to know that perception is reliable.

Unsurprisingly, this defense of perception has come under considerable fire. The epistemologist William Alston puts the central point nicely:

> *If sense perception is reliable*, a track record argument will suffice to show that it is.... But ... the argument will not do its job unless we *are* justified in accepting its premises; and that is the case only if sense perception is in fact reliable. This is to offer a stone instead of bread.... We can just as well say

4. As far as I know, van Cleve pioneered this idea in his paper on Descartes (van Cleve [1979]). See also Alston [1986].

of crystal ball gazing that if it *is* reliable, we can use a track record argument to show that it is reliable. But when we ask whether one or another source of belief is reliable, we are interested in *discriminating* those that can reasonably be trusted from those that cannot. Hence merely showing that *if* a given source is reliable it can be shown by its record to be reliable, does nothing to indicate that the source belongs with the sheep rather than with the goats. (Alston [1993], p. 17)

The Plain Inquirer would lodge a nearby complaint. She's prepared to allow that the Plain Man might 'know', in the externalist's sense, that perception is reliable on the basis of this sort of reasoning, but her ambitions are higher: she doesn't just want this bare sort of 'knowledge'; she wants a comprehensive understanding of when and how she's able to gain information about the world by perception.[5] To satisfy that ambition, it isn't enough that perception in fact be reliable; she needs to understand how and why it is. That's why her assessment of perception isn't a mere track record argument, but a detailed, multidisciplinary effort, with inputs ranging from her physical theory of the surrounding objects, the optics of light, reflection and refraction, the physiology and psychology of the visual system, the neurological structure of the visual cortex and other contributing areas of the brain, and so on. This effort will, inevitably, appeal to perceptual evidence, displaying a kind of circularity—and she can't remove that circularity by externalistic means without giving up the game.

Still, it's important to notice that the Plain Inquirer's investigation of perception is an assessment, not a foregone conclusion. Vision theory begins from ordinary perceptual evidence, but it progresses to a full analysis of how the visual system works in optimal conditions, which conditions are suboptimal and why, and what kinds of errors we're prone to—from small

5. Stroud [1994] also objects that externalism, even if it's true, doesn't answer the question he's asking, but Stroud's question appears to be either the 'from scratch' challenge (from Lecture I) or the 'infer from inner to outer' challenge (from Lecture II), not the Plain Inquirer's ordinary project.

correctable aberrations in her original perceptual evidence, to familiar optical illusions, to quite surprising discoveries like inattentional and change blindness.[6] The result is both a deep respect for the feats the system accomplishes and a chastened sense of how the very mechanisms that enable those feats also produce previously unimagined failures. So the kind of circularity involved in this assessment isn't the kind that ensures success; it isn't true that starting from perception guarantees that perception will turn out to be reliable.

In the end, the Plain Inquirer's investigation yields what Alston calls 'significant self-support':

> Our scientific account of perceptual processes shows how it is that sense experience serves as a sensitive indicator of certain kinds of facts about the environment of the perceiver. (Alston [1993], p. 138)

He recognizes that this has considerable force:

> These results are by no means trivial. . . . It is quite conceivable that . . . [the] output of [sense perception] . . . should not have put us in a position to acquire enough understanding of the workings of perception to see why it can be relied on. (Ibid.)

And though there is circularity here, this approach, unlike the track-record argument, does separate sheep from goats: the scientific account

> is still infected with epistemic circularity; apart from reliance on [sense perception] we have . . . no way of confirming our suppositions about the workings of perception. Nevertheless, this is not the trivial epistemically circular support that necessarily extends to every practice, the automatic

---

6. See, e.g., Palmer [1999], pp. 536–539. In one dramatic experiment, subjects attending to a basketball passing drill failed to notice when a gorilla (actually, a woman in a gorilla suit) 'walked from right to left . . . stopped in the middle of the players as the action continued all around it, turned to face the camera, thumped its chest, then resumed walking across the screen' (Simons and Chabris [1999], p. 1069).

confirmation of each output by itself. Many ... practices, like crystal-ball gazing, do not show anything analogous to [these] results. (Ibid.)

So the form of circularity we now face isn't the blatant circularity of including the conclusion among the premises, nor is it the less serious but still troublesome circularity of the externalist's track-record argument.

By this route, we've reached the core question: what epistemological disadvantage *does* the Plain Inquirer's brand of circularity suffer from? Alston puts it this way:

> There is, perhaps, no particular assumption that cannot be disengaged and successfully argued for, but we cannot turn the trick with the whole lot all at once. (Alston [1986], p. 347)

'Turning the trick on the whole lot all at once' is a nice phrase for the 'from scratch' challenge. Though this 'has fatal implications for certain traditional aspirations', Alston doesn't think we need succumb to the 'depths of despair' (ibid., p. 346):

> This may be a severe blow to philosophical pride, but by the same token it is a salutary lesson in intellectual humility. (Ibid., p. 347)

Here Alston aligns with the Plain Inquirer and her fellow travelers (Reid, Moore): the 'from scratch' challenge can't be answered, but ordinary evidence retains its force. From the Plain Inquirer's point of view, then, the skeptical argument based on Agrippa's trilemma collapses into the 'from scratch' challenge of Lecture I.

APPENDIX B

The Closure Argument

In contemporary discussions, Moore's argument in 'Proof of an external world' is often boiled down to a bare schematic inference from his knowledge of his hands to his knowledge of the external world—where that conclusion is taken as a refutation of 'from scratch' skepticism, equivalent to the claim that I know I'm not extraordinary dreaming. The line goes something like this:

(1) I know this a hand.
(2) If this is a hand, then I'm not extraordinary dreaming.
(3) Therefore, I know I'm not extraordinary dreaming.

The skeptic then converts Moore's modus ponens into a modus tollens:[1]

---

1. In his other anti-skeptical writings, especially Moore [1944], Moore exploits this modus ponens/modus tollens duality with a comparative challenge: consider any argument that concludes 'I don't know this is a hand'; an equally cogent argument runs from 'I know this is a hand' to the negation of that argument's premises; now ask which of the two—the modus ponens or the modus tollens—has more

(i) I don't know I'm not extraordinary dreaming.

(ii) If this is a hand, then I'm not extraordinary dreaming.

(iii) Therefore, I don't know this is a hand.

I hope what's gone before has demonstrated that both the Dream Argument and Moore's anti-skeptical views are more subtle and interesting than this, but let's set that aside and consider the contemporary skeptical argument (i)–(iii) on its own terms.

Many anti-skeptics—unimpressed by (1)–(3),[2] but bothered by (i)–(iii)—respond by attempting to deny (i), by attempting to show that I know I'm not extraordinary dreaming . . . or deceived by an Evil Demon or a brain in a mad neuroscientist's vat. (As we've seen, the Plain Man and the Plain Inquirer take this for a lost cause.) The so-called Closure Argument focuses instead on the role of (ii). The first observation is that (iii) doesn't follow from (ii) alone, that I have to be aware of the logical connection in (ii), so let's make that assumption. The second observation is that (iii) doesn't follow unless knowledge is closed under implication, unless my knowing q follows from my knowing p and my knowing p implies q. So this debate between the skeptic and the anti-skeptic becomes a debate over Closure.

Though it seems obvious at first blush, Closure is actually a tricky principle. For example, recall (from I.3) Austin's remark on what it takes to know there's a goldfinch in the garden:

> Enough is enough: it doesn't mean everything. Enough means enough to show that (within reason, and for present intents and purposes) it 'can't' be anything else . . . it doesn't mean, for example, enough to show that it isn't a stuffed goldfinch. (Austin [1946], p. 84)

plausible premises. Lycan [2007] and Weatherall [201?] develop this Moorean line of thought.

2. Dretske [2005], p. 24, calls (1)–(3) 'chutzpah, not philosophy'.

Suppose I know that it's a goldfinch; does it follow that I know it's not a stuffed goldfinch? Some take Austin to say yes;[3] some take him to say no;[4] perhaps he'd say that sometimes words fail us.[5] Among contemporary epistemologists, many assume that a satisfactory account of knowledge must ratify Closure, while others offer accounts that don't.[6] This is naturally intertwined with the contemporary debate over the concept of knowledge.

Fortunately, there's another way of approaching this skeptical argument. What makes Closure compelling, after all, is the thought that if p implies q, then any evidence I have for p ought to serve just as well as evidence for q. Focusing then on the matter of evidence, the question is whether Moore's evidence for the existence of his hands 'transmits' across the inference to the conclusion that he's not extraordinary dreaming. Closure might be correct—if Moore knows he has hands, it might also be true that he knows he's not extraordinary dreaming—but the evidence still not transmit; it could be that his knowledge that he's not extraordinary dreaming is based on evidence other than the evidence he has for the existence of his hands. The prominent British philosopher Crispin Wright argues that Moore's argument is ineffective independently of Closure, because the evidence[7] doesn't transmit. The idea is this: Moore's evidence for 'here's a hand' is his current sensory experience; that evidence isn't conclusive by itself, its force depends on suitable circumstances (one unsuitable circumstance would be his immersion in an extraordinary dream); so Moore's evidence for his premise only has force if his conclusion is true.

3. E.g., Leite [2011].
4. E.g., Kaplan [2011].
5. See footnote 48 of Lecture I.
6. See Steup [2005], pp. 1–4, for an overview. Turri [2015] conducts some careful surveys and determines that ordinary practice with the word 'know' actually varies on this point.
7. Wright [2002] actually employs a more technical notion—'defeasible warrant'—and others prefer 'justification'. I think these subtle differences can be safely ignored for present purposes.

Given this logical structure, Moore's evidence for his premise can't transmit to his conclusion.[8]

This version of Wright's objection seems to rest on the assumption that Moore's evidence for his hands involves an argument from inner to outer, but I think this isn't essential.[9] Whatever evidence Moore has for his hands—even the Plain Inquirer's complex style of evidence—will fail to transmit to his conclusion for a very simple reason: insofar as the skeptical hypotheses—extraordinary dreaming, the Evil Demon, the Brain in the Vat—are expressly designed to pose the 'from scratch' challenge, they are by their very nature structurally impervious to evidence. Of course Moore, as I've been understanding him, is perfectly aware of this fact and doesn't claim to have refuted the skeptical hypothesis. What he does is provide a store of ordinary evidence and (implicitly) challenge the skeptic to explain why it's invalidated by the absence of extraordinary evidence.

In sum, then, if my evidence for the existence of my hands doesn't transmit to the conclusion that I'm not extraordinary dreaming, then the fact that I have no evidence that I'm not extraordinary dreaming doesn't imply

---

8. Oddly enough, Wright suggests that Moore's argument fails to transmit because it occurs in a particular rhetorical context: for his argument to successfully transmit, 'Moore would need independent information that experience of the kind he is having is unlikely to occur unless there is a material world [or] independent information . . . that there is a material world. Moore cannot, in the dialectical setting which he has undertaken—one of trying to marshal a response to skepticism—take it for granted that he has either of those pieces of information' (Wright [2002], p. 337). In fact, it seems to me that one of the most effective moves Moore makes in 'Proof' is to reverse this very dialectical arrow: the skepticism debate so often begins with the skeptic in possession, using a skeptical hypothesis to pose a skeptical challenge; Moore places himself (and the Plain Inquirer) in possession and issues a(n implicit) challenge to the skeptic. The only mention of any skeptical argument at all comes at the very end of the paper, where Moore admits that he hasn't proved he's not dreaming. Weatherall [201?] makes this point in the process of arguing for a different, quite intriguing, reading of 'Proof' as a stage in Moore's comparative anti-skeptical reasoning (sketched in footnote 1).

9. Wright apparently agrees. He gives a second version of the argument for those who think perception is 'direct'.

that I have no evidence for the existence of my hands. This leaves room for the Plain Inquirer (and Moore as I read him) to hold that she has evidence for the existence of her hands but no evidence that she's not extraordinary dreaming. I leave the question of Closure and the concept of knowledge to the epistemologists.

BIBLIOGRAPHY

Alexander, Joshua [2012] *Experimental Philosophy* (Cambridge: Polity).

Alston, William [1986] 'Epistemic circularity', reprinted in his *Epistemic Justification* (Ithaca, NY: Cornell University Press, 1989), pp. 319–349.

———. [1993] *The Reliability of Sense Perception* (Ithaca, NY: Cornell University Press).

Austin, J. L. [1939] 'Are there *a priori* concepts?', reprinted in his [1979], pp. 32–54.

———. [1940] 'The meaning of a word', reprinted in his [1979], pp. 55–75.

———. [1946] 'Other minds', reprinted in his [1979], pp. 76–116.

———. [1955] *How to Do Things with Words*, second edition, J. O. Urmson and M. Sbisà, eds. (Cambridge, MA: Harvard University Press, 1962).

———. [1956] 'A plea for excuses', reprinted in his [1979], pp. 175–204.

———. [1956a] 'Ifs and cans', reprinted in his [1979], pp. 205–232.

———. [1958] *Lectures at the University of California, Berkeley*, notes of R. Lawrence and W. Hayes, with supplements from W. Matson.

———. [1962] *Sense and Sensabilia* (Oxford: Oxford University Press).

———. [1979] *Philosophical Papers*, third edition, J. O. Urmson and G. J. Warnock, eds. (Oxford: Oxford University Press).

Ayer, A. J. [1940] *The Foundations of Empirical Knowledge* (London: MacMillan).

Baker, G. P., and P. M. S. Hacker [2005] *Wittgenstein: Understanding and Meaning*, second, extensively revised edition (Malden, MA: Blackwell).

Barnes, Jonathan [1982] 'The beliefs of a Pyrrhonist', reprinted in M. Burnyeat and M. Frede, eds., *The Original Sceptics: A Controversy* (Indianapolis, IN: Hackett, 1998), pp. 58–91.

Baz, Avner [2012] *When Words Are Called For: A Defense of Ordinary Language Philosophy* (Cambridge, MA: Harvard University Press).

Bennett, Jonathan [1971] *Locke, Berkeley, Hume* (Oxford: Oxford University Press).

Berkeley, George [1709] *An Essay towards a New Theory of Vision*, reprinted in C. Turbayne, ed., *Works on Vision, George Berkeley* (Indianapolis, IN: Bobbs-Merrill, 1963), pp. 7–102.

———. [1710] *A Treatise Concerning the Principles of Human Knowledge*, J. Dancy, ed. (Oxford: Oxford University Press, 1998).

———. [1713] *Three Dialogues between Hylas and Philonous*, J. Dancy, ed. (Oxford: Oxford University Press, 1998).

———. [1948] *The Works of George Berkeley, Bishop of Cloyne*, A. A. Luce and T. E. Jessop, eds., volume 2 (London: Nelson and Sons).

Broughton, Janet [1983] 'Hume's skepticism about causal inference', *Pacific Philosophical Quarterly* 64, pp. 3–18.

———. [2002] *Descartes's Method of Doubt* (Princeton, NJ: Princeton University Press).

———. [2003] 'Hume's naturalism about cognitive norms', *Philosophical Topics* 31, pp. 1–19.

Crone, Robert [1992] 'The history of stereoscopy', *Documenta Ophthamologica* 81, pp. 1–16.

de Bary, Philip [2002] *Thomas Reid and Skepticism* (London: Routledge).

Dedekind, Richard [1872] 'Continuity and irrational numbers', in W. Ewald, ed., *From Kant to Hilbert*, volume II, W. W. Beman and W. Ewald, trans. (Oxford: Oxford University Press, 1996), pp. 765–779.

Dennett, Daniel [1991] *Consciousness Explained* (Boston: Little, Brown).

Descartes, René [1630] 'Letter to Mersenne, 27 May 1630', in his [1991], pp. 25–26.

———. [1632?] *Optics*, in P. Olscamp, ed. and trans., *Discourse on Method, Optics, Geometry and Meteorology*, revised edition (Indianapolis, IN: Hackett, 2001), pp. 65–173.

———. [1633?] *Treatise of Man*, T. S. Hall, trans. and ed. (Amherst, NY: Prometheus Books, 2003). First published posthumously in 1664.

———. [1641] *Meditations on First Philosophy*, in his [1984], pp. 1–62.

———. [1641a] 'Letter to Mersenne, 28 January 1641', in his [1991], pp. 171–173.

———. [1642] *Objections and Replies*, in his [1984], pp. 66–383.

———. [1644] 'Letter to Mesland, 2 May 1644', in his [1991], pp. 231–236.

———. [1984] *The Philosophical Writings of Descartes*, volume II, J. Cottingham et al., eds. (Cambridge: Cambridge University Press).

———. [1991] *The Philosophical Writings of Descartes*, volume III, J. Cottingham et al., eds. (Cambridge: Cambridge University Press).

Diamond, Cora [1986] 'Realism and the realistic spirit', reprinted in her *The Realistic Spirit* (Cambridge, MA: MIT Press, 1991), pp. 39–72.

Downing, Lisa [1998] 'The status of mechanism in Locke's Essay', *Philosophical Review* 107, pp. 381–414.

Dretske, Fred [2005] 'The case against closure', in Steup and Sosa [2005], pp. 13–26, 43–46.

Einstein, Albert [1961] *Relativity* (New York: Crown).

Feynman, Richard [1985] *Surely You're Joking, Mr. Feynman!* (New York: W. W. Norton).

Filevich, Elisa, Martin Dresler, Timothy Brick, and Simone Kühn [2015] 'Metacognitive mechanisms underlying lucid dreaming', *The Journal of Neuroscience* 35, pp. 1082–1088.

Fischer, Eugen [2011] *Philosophical Delusion and Its Therapy* (New York: Routledge).

Fogelin, Robert [1976] *Wittgenstein*, first edition (London: Routledge).

———. [1987] *Wittgenstein*, second edition (London: Routledge).

Frankfurt, Harry [1977] 'Descartes and the creation of the eternal truths', *Philosophical Review* 86, pp. 36–57.

Garber, Daniel [1986] 'Semel in Vita: The scientific background to Descartes' *Meditations*', reprinted in his *Descartes Embodied* (Cambridge: Cambridge University Press, 2001), pp. 221–256.

Gettier, Edmund [1963] 'Is justified true belief knowledge?', *Analysis* 23, pp. 121–123.

Grice, Paul [1958] 'Postwar Oxford philosophy', reprinted in his [1989], pp. 171–180.

———. [1967] 'Logic and conversation', in his [1989], pp. 1–143.

———. [1987] 'Conceptual analysis and the province of philosophy', in his [1989], pp. 181–185.

———. [1987a] 'Retrospective epilogue', in his [1989], pp. 339–385.

———. [1989] *Studies in the Way of Words* (Cambridge, MA: Harvard University Press).

Grice, Paul, and P. F. Strawson [1956] 'In defense of a dogma', reprinted in Grice [1989], pp. 196–212.

Gusstafsson, Martin, and Richard Sørli, eds. [2011] *The Philosophy of J. L. Austin* (Oxford: Oxford University Press).

Harris, Stephen [1997] 'Berkeley's argument from perceptual relativity', *History of Philosophy Quarterly* 14, pp. 99–120.

Hatfield, Gary [1993] 'Reason, nature, and God in Descartes', in S. Voss, ed., *Essays on the Philosophy and Science of René Descartes* (New York: Oxford University Press), pp. 259–287.

———. [2002] 'Perception as unconscious inference', reprinted in his [2009a], pp. 124–152.

———. [2009] 'On perceptual constancy', in his [2009a], pp. 178–211.

———. [2009a] *Perception and Cognition* (Oxford: Oxford University Press).

———. [2015] 'Natural geometry in Descartes and Kepler', *Res Philosophica* 92, pp. 117–148.

Hatfield, Gary, and Sarah Allred, eds. [2012] *Visual Experience: Sensation, Cognition and Constancy* (Oxford: Oxford University Press).

Hatfield, Gary, and William Epstein [1979] "The sensory core and the medieval foundations of early modern vision theory', reprinted in Hatfield [2009], pp. 358–387.

Hockney, David [2006] *Secret Knowledge: Rediscovering the Lost Techniques of the Old Masters*, revised and expanded edition (New York: Penguin Group).

Hume, David [1739] *A Treatise of Human Nature*, D. And M. Norton, eds. (Oxford: Oxford University Press, 2000).

———. [1748] *An Enquiry Concerning Human Understanding*, T. Beauchamp, ed. (Oxford: Oxford University Press, 1999).

Kant, Immanuel [1781/7] *Critique of Pure Reason*, P. Guyer and A. Wood, trans. and eds. (Cambridge: Cambridge University Press, 1997).

Kaplan, Mark [2011] 'Tales of the unknown: Austin and the argument from ignorance', in Gutafsson and Sørli [2011], pp. 51 77.

Klein, Peter [1999] 'Human knowledge and the infinite regress of reasons', *Philosophical Perspectives* 13, pp. 297–325.

Kornblith, Hilary [2002] *Knowledge and Its Place in Nature* (Oxford: Oxford University Press).

———. [2007] 'Naturalism and intuitions', *Grazer Philosophische Studien* 74, pp. 27–49.

Kripke, Saul [1982] *Wittgenstein on Rules and Private Language* (Cambridge, MA: Harvard University Press).

Kusch, Martin [2006] *A Sceptical Guide to Meaning and Rules: Defending Kripke's Wittgenstein* (Montreal: McGill-Queen's University Press).

Lawlor, Krista [2013] *Assurance: An Austinian View of Knowledge and Knowledge Claims* (Oxford: Oxford University Press).

Leite, Adam [2011] 'Austin, dreams, and skepticism', in Gustafsson and Sørli [2011], pp. 78–113.

Lindberg, David [1976] *Theories of Vision from Al-Kindi to Kepler* (Chicago: University of Chicago Press).

Locke, John [1689] *An Essay Concerning Human Understanding*, P. Niddich, ed. (Oxford: Oxford University Press, 1975).

Lycan, William [2007] 'Moore's anti-skeptical strategies', in S. Nuccetelli and G. Seay, eds., *Themes from G. E. Moore* (Oxford: Oxford University Press), pp. 84–99.

Maddy, Penelope [2007] *Second Philosophy* (Oxford: Oxford University Press).

———. [2011] *Defending the Axioms* (Oxford: Oxford University Press).

———. [2011a] 'Naturalism and common sense' (Hume and Reid), *Analytic Philosophy* 52, pp. 481–504.

———. [2011b] 'Naturalism, transcendentalism, and therapy', in J. Smith and P. Sullivan, eds., *Transcendental Philosophy and Naturalism* (Oxford: Oxford University Press), pp. 120–156.

———. [2014] *The Logical Must* (New York: Oxford University Press).

———. [2014a] 'A second philosophy of logic', in P. Rush, ed., *The Metaphysics of Logic* (Cambridge: Cambridge University Press), pp. 93–108.

Marr, David [1982] *Vision* (Cambridge, MA: MIT Press, 2010).

Metzinger, Thomas, ed. [2000] *Neural Correlates of Consciousness* (Cambridge, MA: MIT Press).

Miller, Alexander, and Crispin Wright, eds. [2002] *Rule-following and Meaning* (Montreal: McGill-Queen's University Press).

Moore, G. E. [1903] *Principia Ethica* (Cambridge: Cambridge University Press).

———. [1925] 'Defence of common sense', reprinted in his [1959], pp. 32–59.

———. [1933/4] 'Selections from a course of lectures given in 1933–34', in C. Lewy, ed., *Lectures on Philosophy by G. E. Moore* (London: George Allen and Unwin, 1966), pp. 151–196.

———. [1939] 'Proof of an external world', reprinted in his [1959], pp. 127–150.

———. [1944] 'Four forms of scepticism', lecture revised and published in his [1959], pp. 196–226.

———. [1957] 'Visual sense data', reprinted in R. Swartz, ed., *Perceiving, Sensing, and Knowing* (Berkeley: University of California Press, 1965), pp. 130–137.

———. [1959] *Philosophical Papers* (London: Allen and Unwin).

Moyal-Sharrock, Danièlle, ed. [2004] *The Third Wittgenstein: The Post-Investigations* (Burlington, VT: Ashgate).

Nichols, Ryan [2007] *Thomas Reid's Theory of Perception* (Oxford: Oxford University Press).

Palmer, Stephen [1999] *Vision Science* (Cambridge, MA: MIT Press).

Pitcher, George [1977] *Berkeley* (London: Routledge and Kegan Paul).

Putnam, Hilary [1981] 'Brains in a vat', in his *Reason, Truth and History* (Cambridge: Cambridge University Press), pp. 1–21, reprinted in K. DeRose and T. Warfield, eds., *Skepticism* (New York, NY: Oxford University Press, 1999), pp. 27–42.

Quine, W. V. O. [1948] 'On what there is', reprinted in his [1980], pp. 1–19.

———. [1951] 'Two dogmas of empiricism', reprinted in his [1980], pp. 20–46.

———. [1969] 'Natural kinds', in his *Ontological Relativity* (New York: Columbia University Press), pp. 114–138.

———. [1980] *From a Logical Point of View*, second edition (Cambridge, MA: Harvard University Press).

Reid, Thomas [1764] *An Inquiry into the Human Mind on the Principles of Common Sense*, D. Brookes, ed. (University Park: Pennsylvania State University Press, 1997).

———. [1785] *Essays on the Intellectual Powers of Man*, D. Brookes, ed. (University Park: Pennsylvania State University Press, 2002).

Rickless, Samuel [1997] 'Locke on primary and secondary qualities', *Pacific Philosophical Quarterly* 78, pp. 297–319.

Rogers, Brian [2011] *Philosophical Method in Wittgenstein's On Certainty*, PhD dissertation, University of California, Irvine.

Russell, Bertrand [1912] *The Problems of Philosophy* (London: Williams and Norgate).

———. [1959] *My Philosophical Development* (Oxford: Routledge).

Saunders, Simon, Jonathan Barrett, Adrian Kent, and David Wallace, eds. [2010] *Many Worlds?: Everett, Quantum Theory, and Reality* (Oxford: Oxford University Press).

Schuhmann, Karl, and Barry Smith [1990] 'Elements of speech act theory in the work of Thomas Reid', *History of Philosophy Quarterly* 7, pp. 47–66.

Schwitzgebel, Eric [2011] 'The unreliability of naïve introspection', in his *Perplexities of Consciousness* (Cambridge, MA: MIT Press), pp. 117–137.

Sextus Empiricus [2000] *Outlines of Scepticism*, J. Annas and J. Barnes, trans. and eds. (Cambridge: Cambridge University Press, 2000).

Simons, Daniel, and Christopher Chabris [1999] 'Gorillas in our midst: Sustained inattentional blindness for dynamic events', *Perception* 28, pp. 1059–1074.

Soames, Scott [2003] *Philosophical Analysis in the Twentieth* Century, volume 2, *The Age of Meaning* (Princeton, NJ: Princeton University Press).

Sosa, Ernest [2009] 'Reflective knowledge in the best circles', chapter 9 of his *Reflective Knowledge* (Oxford: Oxford University Press), pp. 178–210.

Spoormaker, Victor, and Jan van den Bout [2006] 'Lucid dreaming treatment for nightmares', *Psychotherapy and Psychosomatics* 75, pp. 389–394.

Stern, David [2004] *Wittgenstein's Philosophical Investigations* (Cambridge: Cambridge University Press).

Steup, Matthais [2005] 'Introduction to Part I,' in Steup and Sosa [2005], pp. 1–12.

Steup, Matthais, and Ernest Sosa [2005] *Contemporary Debates in Epistemology* (Malden, MA: Blackwell).

Strawson, P. F. [1985] *Skepticism and Naturalism* (New York: Columbia University Press).

Stroll, Avrum [1994] *Moore and Wittgenstein on Certainty* (New York: Oxford University Press).

Stroud, Barry [1977] *Hume* (London: Routledge and Kegan Paul).

———. [1984] *The Significance of Philosophical Scepticism* (Oxford: Oxford University Press).

————. [1994] 'Scepticism, "externalism", and the goal of epistemology', reprinted in his [2000], pp. 139–154.

————. [1996] 'Epistemological reflection on knowledge of the external world', reprinted in his [2000], pp. 122–138.

————. [2000] *Understanding Human Knowledge* (Oxford: Oxford University Press).

————. [2009] 'Scepticism and the senses', *European Journal of Philosophy* 17, pp. 559–570.

Turri, John [2015] 'An open and shut case: epistemic closure in the manifest image', *Philosopher's Imprint* 15, pp. 1–18.

Turri, John, and Peter Klein, eds. [2014] *Ad Infinitum: New Essays on Epistemological Infinitism* (Oxford: Oxford University Press).

Urmson, J. O. [1969] 'Austin's philosophy', in K. T. Fann, ed., *Symposium on J. L. Austin* (London: Routledge and Kegan Paul), pp. 22–32.

Van Cleve, James [1979] 'Foundationalism, epistemic principles, and the Cartesian Circle', *Philosophical Review* 88, pp. 55–91.

Voss, Ursula, Romain Holzmann, Inka Tuin, and J. Allan Hobson [2009] 'Lucid dreaming: A state of consciousness with features of both waking and non-lucid dreaming', *Sleep* 32, pp. 1191–1200.

Warnock, G. J. [1973] 'Saturday mornings', in I. Berlin et al., eds., *Essays on J. L. Austin* (Oxford: Oxford University Press), pp. 31–45.

Weatherall, James [201?] 'On G. E. Moore's "Proof of an external world" ', to appear in *Pacific Philosophical Quarterly*.

Weinberg, Jonathan, Shaun Nichols, and Stephen Stich [2001] 'Normativity and epistemic intuitions', reprinted in J. Knobe and S. Nichols, eds., *Experimental Philosophy* (New York: Oxford University Press, 2008), pp. 17–45.

Weschler, Lawrence [1984] 'Cameraworks: Staring down a paralyzed cyclops', reprinted in his *True to Life: Twenty-five Years of Conversations with David Hockney* (Berkeley: University of California Press, 2008), pp. 1–51.

Williams, Michael [1996] *Unnatural Doubts* (Princeton, NJ: Princeton University Press).

Wilson, Margaret [1992] 'Descartes on the perception of primary qualities', reprinted in her *Ideas and Mechanism* (Princeton, NJ: Princeton University Press, 1999), pp. 26–40.

Wilson, Mark [2006] *Wandering Significance* (Oxford: Oxford University Press).

Wittgenstein, Ludwig [1922] *Tractatus Logico-Philosophicus*, D. F. Pears and B. F. McGuiness, trans. (London: Routledge and Kegan Paul, 1961).

———. [1933/34] *The Blue Book*, in *The Blue and Brown Books* (New York: Harper and Row, 1958), pp. 1–74.

———. [1934/35] 'Lectures, 1934–35', in *Wittgenstein's Lectures, Cambridge, 1932–1935* (Amherst, NY: Prometheus Books, 2001), pp. 75–201.

———. [1953] *Philosophical Investigations*, fourth edition, G. E. M. Anscombe, P. M. S. Hacker, and J. Shulte, trans. (Oxford: Blackwell, 2009).

———. [1969] *On Certainty*, G. E. M. Anscombe and G. H. von Wright, trans. and eds. (Oxford: Blackwell).

———. [1978] *Remarks on the Foundations of Mathematics*, revised edition, G. E. M. Anscombe, trans., G. H. von Wright, R. Rhees, and G. E. M. Anscombe, eds. (Cambridge, MA: MIT Press).

———. [2011] *Ludwig Wittgenstein: Complete Correspondence*, Innsbrucker electronic edition.

Wright, Crispin [2002] '(Anti-)sceptics simple and subtle: G. E. Moore and John McDowell', *Philosophy and Phenomenological Research* 65, pp. 330–348.

Zadra, Antonio, D. C. Donderi, and Robert Pihl [1992] 'Efficacy of lucid dream induction for lucid and non-lucid dreamers', *Dreaming* 2, pp. 85–97

INDEX

DISCARD